S. Cooper

An Essay on the Resumption of Specie Payments

Compared with an Irredeemable Paper Currency, and...

S. Cooper

An Essay on the Resumption of Specie Payments
Compared with an Irredeemable Paper Currency, and...

ISBN/EAN: 9783744721295

Printed in Europe, USA, Canada, Australia, Japan

Cover: Foto ©Suzi / pixelio.de

More available books at **www.hansebooks.com**

AN ESSAY

ON THE

RESUMPTION OF SPECIE PAYMENTS

COMPARED WITH AN

IRREDEEMABLE PAPER CURRENCY,

AND THE

EFFECTS OF OUR FOREIGN INDEBTEDNESS UPON COMMERCE, BUSINESS, AND
MONEY DISTRIBUTION; WITH COMMENTS UPON THE SPEECH OF
SENATOR JONES, OF NEVADA, AND THE OPEN LETTER OF
REV. DR. BACON, OF YALE UNIVERSITY, UPON
THE NATIONAL FINANCES.

By S. COOPER.

SAN FRANCISCO:

PRINTED BY THE PRINTING AND LITHOGRAPHING DEPARTMENT OF A. L. BANCROFT & CO.

1874.

PREFACE.

THIS Essay was originally designed as a newspaper article; but, growing out of proportions adapted to that purpose, it is in its present form respectfully dedicated to the attention amd impartial judgment of the American people, whose prosperity it is designed to promote, by the

AUTHOR.

EUREKA, HUMBOLDT CO., CAL.

RESUMPTION OF SPECIE PAYMENTS.

" Concerning the propriety of the ultimate and even speedy resumption of specie payments, there is scarcely a dissenting voice, either among the people or the Press." " Upon one point only has there been unanimity—it is the desirability of specie payments."

THE above sentences are taken from two articles in the *Republic* for February, 1874. They indicate a very general, a nearly unanimous, argreement in favor of resumption. I dissent. Resumption would be unwise, even if it could be easily and readily accomplished, and if its accomplishment would not immediately be detrimental to the business of the country; and I propose to give some reasons for this opinion.

It may be well here to inquire what is meant by "resumption of specie payments." Does it mean that the Government shall receive and disburse nothing but coin? It has never suspended the receipt of coin for custom duties, nor the disbursement of coin for the interest on its bonds. Since the issuance of the national currency, it has never redeemed any in specie (except in the way of selling gold), and it cannot be said that specie payment of the currency can be resumed, when it has never been begun. The national banks never have paid specie for their notes. How, then, can they *resume* specie payments? They may redeem their notes in specie; that would be redemption, not resumption.

The phrase is borrowed from the old banks. They suspended specie payments and resumed specie payments. Under the former bank system, bank suspension of specie payments and business panic and general bankruptcy were simultaneous. So, also, were the resumption of specie payments and the revival of business. These phrases, the "suspension of specie payments," and the "resumption of specie payments," have not only come to us from the old bank system, but have brought with them the ideas with which they had become associated in the public mind. The literature of finance and political economy, the history of banks and business, and the experiences of the people, had all confirmed the association in the public mind, of the suspension of specie payments by the banks, with business depression and prevalent bankruptcy, and the resumption of specie payments with business prosperity. They are phrases fraught with an association of ideas, growing out of an association of facts and experiences. Therefore, the phrases "a return to specie payments," "the resumption of specie payments," convey to most minds the ideas of business prosperity, steadiness and permanence, and are cited as showing the only solid foundation on which business can be conducted. Hence, the apparent unanimity in favor of the ultimate or even speedy resumption of specie payments.

If it were desirable to resume specie payments the method of its accomplishment would be a subject of serious consideration. The resumptionists have presented no plan that meets with general support among themselves, though a great many have been suggested. All the plans proposed either contemplate contraction or would have that effect. I now propose one which I have not yet seen proposed, which would neither require nor effect a contraction of the currency, viz: Let the tariff on imports be raised fifty per cent. This would approximate the par values of gold and currency; and if not sufficiently effective to bring them together, let the tariff be raised still higher. That result would be certain to follow. It is not my design here to show how this measure would accomplish the end in view, further than to say, that it would be a simple and efficient means to bring together the par values of gold and currency, inasmuch as a check upon foreign importations would turn foreign exchange in our favor and effect a decline in the price of gold. This method of effecting resumption would be opposed by the free trade resumptionists, and by certain interests and sections, on the ground that it favored certain sections and industries at the expense of others. But while it is not likely to be adopted as a matter of choice, if resumption be brought about by any other method, it will have to be resorted to as a matter of necessity, to supply the wants of the Government, unless the unpropitious policy be adopted of increasing the revenues by internal taxation.

Supposing the transition complete, in what form should we have resumption? Would the Government establish agencies to redeem its issues in numerous and convenient localities, or only empower Assistant Treasurers to redeem? Would the banks be permitted to redeem their notes in national notes, or would they be required to redeem in gold, and to keep a reserve of gold, thus being transformed into gold banks? Or, would the whole field be surrendered to a system of gold banks, and government notes be withdrawn from circulation? Or, will the tax that killed the old State banks be repealed, and they be revived to supplant the national banks? Resumption implies a new system of finance. What, then, is the new system to be? Shall the change be the least consistent with the fact of resumption, continuing the national notes in circulation and still a legal tender, with a limited bank circulation redeemable in legal tenders, as at present; or, shall resumption be accompanied with a system of free banking, removing the limit of the bank note circulation, with the legal tenders in circulation; or, shall there be free banking, with the legal tenders withdrawn, leaving only gold and silver legal tenders? If we would contemplate the effects of resumption, we must know what is to be substituted for what we have. I shall endeavor to show that resumption, in any form, is undesirable.

The redeemable legal tender system of currency is preferable to a gold, or gold-base currency, because its quantity is more controlable and can be preserved more uniformly the same per capita *through a long period, or continually.*

This gives steadiness of prices for a correspondingly long period, so far as any currency can effect that end, and is in accord with a maxim of finance, viz: "The quantity of the circulating medium determines the prices of exchangeable commodities:" or, more briefly, The quantity of money determines prices.

It is erroneously charged against the currency that it unsettles prices; that thereby it renders futile all business calculations; that it requires wider margins to guard against market perturbations; that these perturbations destroy the habit of dependence upon moderate and uniform rewards of business and industry, fostering a thirst for and developing reckless speculation.

These effects attributed to our irredeemable currency are generally regarded as true without examination, and as inseparable from it, which is an error. They are only attributable to a paper currency when the increase of such currency is more rapid than the ratio of the increase of population. And the same effects follow a correspondingly rapid increase of a metallic currency. The tendency of all former paper currencies, and of our present currency, from the necessities of the Government *during the war* to rapidly enlarge the quantity of the circulating medium, has led to an association of these effects with a paper currency as inseparable attributes. They were inseparable from the old bank issues, because the aggregate quantity of such issues were under no control or limit. Such is not the case with our present currency; that is limited and controlled by Congressional enactment. Therefore, the evils resulting from an unlimited, uncontrolled and rapid increase or diminution of the circulating medium are eliminated from our national currency, and wherever the effects referred to are manifest they can be traced directly to other causes.

We are invited to return to specie payments, as the only

sound foundation for the stability and steadiness of business. This is a fallacy.

*Resumption offers no guaranty for the steadiness of business,
but the contrary.*

A brief reference to past experience will exemplify this.
The old bank system contemplated a direct inflation of the
currency whenever a new bank was chartered, or an old one
enlarged its capital. There was no means of controlling the
volume of the circulating medium. Each State could multiply banks and bank capital at pleasure. Up to the time of
establishing the Independent Treasury system, gold was
useful only as bank reserves and to pay foreign demands.
State, municipal and corporation securities sold abroad, in
addition to the value of our exports, became a fund against
which to draw foreign bills of exchange, to satisfy foreign
demands for our imports. Gold had no purpose to serve
but that of bank reserves, and so long as we could sell securities gold was as easily imported as anything else, to
form reserves for more bank capital and further inflation of
the currency.

The reserves served for three times their amount of circulation, and when that limitation was disregarded the dispropor-
tion was greater. The facility and temptation to inflate the
currency was irresistible; and, consequently, inflation was
the almost ever-constant effect and accompaniment of specie
payments under that system of banking. Alternations of
inflation and contraction followed each other, until the culmination of inflation in 1836, when the whole country was
wild with speculation. Land speculation was never more
rife. Cities grew as if by magic. Manufactures rapidly
multiplied in the Eastern and Middle States, and the whole
known West and Southwest was dotted over with projected
cities (on paper). Commercial, manufacturing and agricultural pursuits were all stimulated to the highest degree
of activity. Prices of all products were high, and importations were immense compared with any previous period, even
to the extent of importing goods and products produced in
superabundance in our own country. Let it not be forgot-
ten that this inflation occurred *during specie payments.*

Every evil attendant upon inflation was attendant upon this. The reaction came in the ever-memorable 1837. Then came suspension of specie payments. Fortunes were leveled to the ground. The wealthy were made bankrupt, and all business was prostrated and stricken with paralysis, from which it but slowly recovered with some alternations through the next six years, when relief came to many from the United States Bankrupt Law of 1841, and to the country by the passage of the tariff of 1842.

From 1843 to 1856 there was a general revival of business, alternating with slight depressions. During this period currency inflation had been going on, while we had specie payments, until its culmination in 1856. The reaction of 1857 was a repetition of 1837, though less severe. The Independent Treasury system established in 1845, requiring as it did a comparatively large amount of coin for the revenues of the government, had the effect, as its friends claimed it would, to check and retard the course of bank inflation. Without this check, the inflation would have been more rapid and the reaction severer. The supply of gold, too, from California served to increase inflation by increasing bank capital, or by increasing the currency by direct circulation, at the same time that it postponed the reaction by furnishing a supply from which the banks could replenish their reserves. But when the supply was checked and the importations increased, after the reduction of the tariff in 1855, reaction became inevitable, and a general prostration, with a temporary suspension of specie payments and the passage of stay-laws by Western legislatures, were the experiences of 1857.

Here, again, inflation accompanied specie payments, and if the country was prosperous, we cannot close our eyes to the fact that an uncontrolled and uncontrollable inflation was also a fact, and entered more largely than specie payments as a cause of the seeming prosperity.

The history of San Francisco, from the discovery of gold to the present time, shows conclusively that a purely metallic currency is not free from inflations and contractions, but more conspicuously was this shown from 1852 to 1857. Up to the spring of 1854, gold had been received from the mines in a constantly increasing quantity. ~~Interest~~ was from three to five per cent. per month. It were an error to infer from this that money was scarce. The plethora of money sustained these high rates, and these high rates caused a plethora of money. Importations were great from the East and foreign countries, and had they been paid for immediately the gold from the mines would have gone abroad. A large quantity was sent from the State; but a large quantity was allowed to remain for loan and investment, to profit by the high rates of interest. This caused an inflation—an increase in the quantity of money. Wages were high and profits were magnificent in 1853. Speculation ran wild, and all speculations seemed to turn out profitably. *The rising tide of prices sustained the high rates of interest.* Ordinary men became prodigies of business foresight, energy, boldness, judgment and success. No magnitude of figures daunted them. They had fifty dollar "slugs" in their pockets, safes, and in bank, equal to any conceivable requirement. Early in 1854 it became evident that the flood-tide could rise no higher. The sudden exit of Harry Meiggs sounded the first note of alarm. The tide began to ebb. Real estate failed to realize anticipated prices. Early in 1855 the larger banks failed and smaller ones soon followed. These events gave impetus to the contraction. Projected improvements were postponed. Unfinished buildings were completed only to remain unoccupied, while others remained unfinished for years. All business languished through 1855, 1856, and 1857. Loans on foreign account were collected as they matured, and investments were turned into money and sent away. The receipts from the mines were largely required to satisfy this demand. Thus, through a prolonged system of depletion, the city and State were left without sufficient money to keep up prices. In 1856 real estate could be bought at an average of one half the prices reigning in 1853 and 1854, and business over the State suffered from a scarcity of money.

These facts are cited to show that a gold currency is attended with fluctuations; and that in whatever form specie payments may come, we have no guaranty from past experience against expansions and contractions of the currency, with all their attendant evils: the very evils so lavishly attributed to our present national currency without justification. A purely metallic currency, however, is out of the question. California is fast changing to a gold note currency, and paper forms the business currency of every advanced civilized nation. Resumption, therefore, means a change from our present irredeemable paper to a gold-base paper currency.

It may be said, that the events cited were exceptional, and peculiar to the early days after the discovery of gold. This answer will not avail. Inflation and contraction have alternately been the monetary conditions of the State, and at the present time it is experiencing an inflation (increase of the currency, if preferred) from the extraordinary yield of the Nevada mines during the past two years, and the extraordinary export of breadstuffs during the same period. Should either of these sources of money suddenly fail, a contraction would be inevitable. Should neither of these sources fail, contraction of the currency and depression of business will certainly follow, from the ever-attendant consequences of inflation of a gold or gold-base currency—excessive importations into the State, causing an unfavorable balance of trade, to pay for which the currency will be sent away in quantity exceeding the supply, thus diminishing the quantity in circulation, thereby depressing business.

The tendency of the precious metals to flow to and from the countries using them as their currency, or the base of their currency, is regarded as an effective cause in equating the commerce of nations, by causing an unfavorable balance of trade to be followed by a favorable balance of trade. But this it does by continually disturbing prices—causing a rise and fall in nominal values in every country having an· extensive foreign commerce.

Gold is a constant traveler to and from all commercial countries. As it flows into a country where it is the base of the currency, its increasing quantity enhances prices, and thereby stimulates production and commercial exchanges, rendering the people prosperous; and as it flows from a country its decreasing quantity depresses prices, discouraging production, obstructing exchanges, paralyzing industry, and diminishing the prosperity of the people. These alternations of business prosperity and adversity are undesirable and what every people seek to avoid. With this end in view, resumptionists wish to return to specie payments. They have learned from former systems that paper issues augmented the evils of fluctuations in the currency. But the paper currency from which they have derived their ideas was a gold-base, non-legal-tender, unlimited paper currency—a currency which gave velocity and momentum to the tides in prices, until they have come to entertain the idea that the property of stimulating these tides is inseparable from paper money.

The greenback currency differs from all former paper money, in being a legal tender—irredeemable—and its quantity determined by statute. It is, therefore, a very different currency, and the full measure of this difference many financiers fail to comprehend. How an irredeemable currency can be superior to a redeemable currency, or why its legal tender character, while itself is irredeemable, is a merit and not a demerit, or how any benefits can be conferred upon the country by these attributes, is more than enters into their philosophy.

It is *because* the greenbacks are *irredeemable*, and *legal tender*, and their *quantity determined by law*, that they constitute a superior currency.

The Government having the power to determine the quantity of the circulating medium, *by maintaining a uniform quantity per capita*, can provide against inflation and contraction more effectually than by any system of currency based upon the precious metals as the only legal tender and measure of nominal values.

Population is the true measure of the quantity of money required. The business of the country has its roots in the wants and supplies of the people. The exchanges to be made are of commodities for use and consumption. These, when the people are in a state of industrial prosperity, always bear a proximate ratio to the population. The capacity to produce, and, consequently the quantity of productions, are in a proximate ratio to the population. The employment of the people and their resources in production,

and the exchange of productions constituting the business
of the country, and these in a given state of prosperity being measured by the population, approximately, therefore
population is the best measure of the business of the country. This may not seem to be borne out when considered
with reference to special localities or pursuits compared
with other localities or pursuits; but with reference to the
country as a whole, compared with itself at different stages
of its growth, it will be found approximately true, or true,
other things being equal. Instead, therefore, of saying that
the quantity of currency should always bear a given ratio to
the population *and business* of the country, it is better to
keep population alone in view, as it is itself the best measure we have of the aggregate of business. The amount of
business cannot be accurately measured, nor the amount of
money required be determined, by the aggregate of nominal
values; because, the more money in circulation, the greater
the nominal values, and the greater the quantity of money
needed.

What is inflation and what is contraction? An increase
of the currency is not necessarily inflation. Such an increase as will not disturb prices is not inflation. An increase of the currency so as to keep pace with the increase
of the population who are to use it, is not inflation. If in
1870 we had a quantity of currency in circulation equal to
$20 *per capita*, amounting in the aggregate to $756,000,000
for a population using it of 37,800,000, and our population
increasing at the rate of two and a half per cent. annually,
shall become 50,000,000 in 1880, requiring $1,000,000,000
of currency to maintain the ratio of $20 per capita, a uni-
form increase of the quantity of the currency to this amount
at that time, cannot properly be called inflation. To issue
currency in greater quantity would be inflation. On the
contrary, if the amount be fixed, without increase or diminution, while population is increasing at the rate of nearly
twenty-five per cent. each decade, that is contraction of the
currency *per capita*, and in process of time has the same effect as a direct contraction of the aggregate, though more
gradual and consequently less severely felt.

The duty of the Government, therefore, having found or

adopted a ratio of currency *per capita,* is to maintain that ratio by increasing the currency as the population using it increases.

Specie payment causes us " to buy dear and sell cheap."

Specie payment suspends the law of supply and demand in its relation to the price of gold and silver.

The currency was highly inflated in 1836 and 1856, and prices were correspondingly high. Foreign imports in those years very largely exceeded our exports. Why was there this excess of imports? Because we had *fixed the price* of gold and silver by making the nominal dollar—the dollar of account—the legal tender dollar, and the coin dollar of the same relative fixed value.

The coin dollar is a fixed quantity of gold or silver. This fixed quantity of gold or silver—articles of commerce—was guaranteed at a given price by specie payments and specie legal tender. The nominal price of these metals could not rise correspondingly with the increasing demand. When our currency from any cause whatever became inflated, and other articles of commerce rose in nominal price, corresponding to .the currency inflation, gold and silver could not rise. They were guaranteed at the same price as before the inflation. Each dollar of account would buy the same weight of gold or silver. If, then, foreign nations poured their products upon our markets and sold them at our inflated prices, for every dollar of our inflated currency or money of account which they received, they were guaranteed a fixed quantity of gold or silver, which quantity was determined independently of our inflated currency. It is self-evident, and history shows, that we purchased most freely when our prices were the highest, giving a fixed quantity of gold and silver for every nominal dollar in the price of the purchase. This is buying dear.

Now let us see how we sell cheap. Suppose a foreign merchant had sold in 1836, or 1856, a cargo of goods in our markets, and received his pay in specie-paying bank currency. The purchaser says to him: We have a great variety of goods in our markets which we would like to sell you;

and as we have patronized you, we should like to have you patronize us in return. We have cotton, tobacco, bread-stuff, and many other agricultural and some manufactured products largely in excess of our demands. Most of these are necessities of your people, and you would do well to take a cargo home with you."

The foreigner replies: "It is true, the goods you have named are necessities of our people, and some of them—cotton, tobacco, and a few others—we must obtain from this country. I notice, however, that the market prices of the articles you have named are all very high. Many of them are higher than in my own country. I have found, by a lit-tle calculation, that breadstuffs can be purchased on the Baltic or Black seas much cheaper than here; indeed, at rates that enable us to import them into my country, and then export them to this country and sell them at a profit. Were your prices reasonable I would, with pleasure, take a return cargo. I may take some cotton and tobacco to sup-ply current wants; but as for the rest, I find it most to my interest to change my bank paper into gold and go to other markets where I can buy cheaper until your surplus pro-ducts come down in price."

The domestic merchant replies: "True, there has been a rise in the prices of those articles, but they are not deemed unreasonably high. There has been a general rise of prices, and it is found that articles of export have not kept pace with the general rise, and particularly as compared with the rise in the prices of imports, they are considered unreasonably low when compared with other things."

" Yes," says the foreigner, "but it is not our concern to compare them with other articles in this market. We are more concerned in comparing them with the prices of the same class of articles in other countries, and we find it is to our advantage to buy elsewhere. When you can sell as cheap as we can buy elsewhere your surplus products will be in demand." Thus, having the option of gold or silver at a fixed price, he leaves our products on our hands.

Such a system of depletion of gold cannot last long. And when we have filled our country to repletion with foreign goods at high prices, and raised the prices of our surplus products until they fail to find a foreign market, and coin is taken instead, bank suspension and panic, and a shrinkage of prices follow. Then our domestic products are forced down to prices which enable them to find a foreign market, and thus we are *compelled to sell cheap*.

An irredeemable currency remedies this by enabling us to sell as well as to buy at our own market prices.

With an irredeemable currency our imports are purchased at currency prices, and are paid for in domestic products at our currency prices as affected by the gold premium.

This may be illustrated by comparing the effect upon the domestic prices of our exportable products in 1836 or 1856, if the currency of those years had been an irredeemable legal tender, and the measure of nominal values—in these respects similar to our present national currency with the effect under a redeemable currency. Pursuing the former illustration, suppose the foreigner had sold his cargo in our market for one hundred thousand dollars. This with a redeemable currency was equal to the same quantity of gold. The tariff duties may be estimated at $25,000, gold value; leaving $75,000, gold for cost of production, transportation and profit. The tariff, being determined previously by enactment, could not rise correspondingly with the rise of prices by inflation, and relatively became lower as they became higher.

Had the currency been irredeemable, the quantity in circulation being the same, the prices of imports would have been the same, and the foreigner would have sold his cargo for $100,000 currency. Estimating the gold premium at forty per cent., as it probably would have been at least, this would have required $35,000 to pay tariff duties, leaving $65,000 to be converted into gold, which gives $46,429— for costs of production, transportation and profit; being $28,571 in gold value less than he would have received with a redeemable currency. A gold premium therefore, would have checked the excessive importations during the years referred to. A gold premium also has the effect, virtually,

2

of raising the tariff correspondingly with the rise of prices by inflation. Let us see how exportable products would have been affected.

The foreigner having sold his cargo and paid his duties, holds the balance in bank-bills convertible into gold on demand. He finds the price of wheat $1.50 a bushel and flour $7.50 per bbl., bank currency price equal to gold. On the Baltic or Black Seas they would cost him including cost of a passage across the ocean in ballast, wheat $1.20 per bushel and flour $6.00 per bbl.—reducing foreign coin to our money denominations. Liverpool, Hamburg and Paris prices ranging in wheat from $1.30 to $1.40 per bushel and flour from $6.50 to $7.00 per bbl. gold price. It is very evident that our prices of wheat and flour prevented their export, and limited sales to the domestic demand, and the foreigner found it to his advantage to turn bank currency into gold and go to the Baltic and Black Seas for a supply of breadstuffs.

If the currency had been irredeemable and gold at a premium of 40 per cent. as supposed, the currency price of our wheat reduced to gold would have been $1.07 per bushel, and of flour per bbl. $5.36. An irredeemable currency therefore would have made it advantageous to the foreigner to purchase his cargo of breadstuffs in our markets at our currency prices. The effect in relation to all other exportable articles is the same, opening for them foreign markets, and effecting an equilibrium of imports and exports without a depression of our market prices to effect this end. Thus are we saved from the necessity of buying dear and selling cheap by an irredeemable currency.

It may be answered that the reduction of the currency price of exportable products only shows that we really sell our products cheap, and that nothing is gained by selling at higher prices in what is called a depreciated currency, and that the difference in the currency and gold prices is the measure of the currency depreciation.

This is a fallacy. It assumes that the consumers of the imported cargo and producers of the exported cargo are not benefited by the gold premium. This assumption cannot be separated from its corollary, that the interests of the foreigner who sold his cargo of imports and purchased his cargo of exports were not injured by the gold premium. Were his interests injured by the gold premium? With a redeemable bank currency his $100,000 less import duties left him $75,000. To pay this in products we could not expect to receive more than they would cost elsewhere, including cost of passage in ballast; wheat $1.20 per bushel, and flour $6.00 per bbl. This would allow him to purchase 62,500 bushel of wheat or 12,500 bbls. of flour. With an irredeemable currency and gold premium and prices as supposed—his $100,000 currency less $35,000 to convert into gold to pay duties would leave him $65,000, which converted into gold is equal to $46,429 which would enable him to purchase 43,400 bushels of wheat at $1.07 (equal to $1.50 currency) or 8662 bbls. of flour at $5.36 gold price (equal to $7.50 currency) or about $28,000 less in gold values than with a redeemable currency. And inasmuch as the consumers of the imports pay the same amount under either condition of the currency it is a benefit in the first instance to the producers of exports, and is shared with the consumers through the operations of the laws of trade, by enabling the export producers to purchase more largely and pay better prices to manufacturing consumers.

The estimates of prices and quantities in the foregoing are only illustrative; though they approximate to the facts. To show, however, that the facts of history sustain the foregoing statements and deductions, the following extracts are taken from the Report of the Secretary of the Treasury for the year 1865 :

"*A Statement of the bank note circulation of the country at various periods of highest and lowest issues prior to the war;*

"January, 1830—$61,324,000	January, 1856—$195,747,950
" 1835—103,692,495	" 1857— 214,778,822
" 1836—140,301,038	" 1858— 155,208,344
" 1837—149,185,890	" 1860— 207,102,000
" 1843— 58,564,000	

"It will be noticed by this statement that the bank note circulation of the United States increased from $61,324,000 to $149,185,890 between the 1st of January, 1830, and the 1st of January, 1837, in which latter year the great financial collapse took place; fell from $149,185,890, in 1837, to $58,564,000 in 1843, and rose to $214,778,822 on the 1st of January, 1857, in which year the next severe crisis occurred ; falling that year to $155,208,344, and rising to $207,1C2,000 on the 1st of January, 1860.   *   *   *   *

"The expansion of 1835 and 1836, ending with the terrible financial coi" lapse of 1837, from the effects of which the country did not rally for years, was the consequence of excessive bank circulation and discounts.

*   *   *   "These were years of great inflation, the effects of which have already been referred to—the revulsion of 1837 not only producing great immediate embarrassment, but a prostration which continued until 1843, at the commencement of which year the bank note circulation amounted only to $58,564,000, deposits to $56,168,000, loans $254,544,000 —flour having declined in New York from $10.25 per barrel on the 1st of January, 1837, to $4.69 on the 1st of January, 1843, and other articles in about the same proportion.

"The reaction in 1857 was severe, but from reasons before stated, less disastrous and protracted."

It will be seen, by the foregoing extract and statistics, that a return to specie payments would be a return to constant vicissitudes in the quantity of money in circulation and monetary conditions.   But even these statistics fail to show the rapidity of the expansions and contractions of the currency.   Nearly all the increase in the quantity of currency occurring from January 1st, 1830, to January 1st, 1837, really occurred in the latter three years after the removal of the government deposits from the United States Bank by Jackson.   And nearly all the contraction, including depreciation, of the currency shown to have occurred in the five years succeeding the 1st of January, 1837, really and virtually occurred within six months from that period, the quantity oscillating near the lower point through the remainder of the five years; and the same is true in relation to the great decline in the price of flour and other products, the decline occurring in the first six months of 1837.

Balance of trade and foreign exchange.

With a gold-base currency, if our imports exceed our exports, exclusive of the precious metals, the excess is a balance of trade against us.   We purchase more than we sell, and the difference is either a gold payment or a gold demand—nearly always the latter.   The precious metals are not regarded as exports or imports, but as payment, because, being the basis of the circulating medium, their exportation or importation has a contrary effect from that of the importation or exportation of any other article of commerce.

During the creation of a foreign debt through an unfavorable balance of trade the country is prosperous. It occurs during inflation of the currency, which gives rise to an expanded system of credit based upon general business prosperity or speculative enterprise. Prices are generally high so as to make our market a good one for foreigners to sell in and a poor one for them to buy in. It is a certain indication that a re-action must come; and if the balance of trade against us be great or long continued, the re-action becomes a calamity. This balance against us being in the form of a demand for gold at a fixed price, when the day of payment comes, the gold, which forms the basis of our currency, is sent abroad, contracting the currency, inducing a panic, a shrinkage of prices and general bankruptcy. At length our market prices reach a point so low that foreigners cannot sell us their products to advantage, thus our imports fall off. At the same time they find their opportunity to buy our products cheap, which increases our exports and turns the balance of trade in our favor, when the current of gold begins to return.

It will be seen by this analysis that the balance of trade in our favor, or against us, is only currency expansion or contraction from another point of view. It will be seen, also, that prosperous business induces a balance of trade against us, and, that with specie payments, we have no means of equating this unfavorable balance of trade except through a serious depression of prices and business, and often through the direful calamity of general bankruptcy.

An unfavorable balance, though in the midst of prosperity, is regarded as undesirable, because it is portentous of business depression through a contraction of the currency: while a balance of trade in our favor is always regarded as desirable, though often brought about by great business depression; because it is a cause, as well as an indication, of an increase of the currency and revival of business.

Sometimes, it is true, that superabundant crops of our staple exports, or unfavorable crops abroad give a balance

of trade in our favor, as in the case of the wheat crop of
California the past two years. But much more is usually
attributed to this cause than is properly due to it. If the
crops in California continue equally abundant they will fail
to give her a favorable balance of trade. They have served
to expand the volume of her currency, which is attended
with increased activity in business, and increasing importations into the State, which will continue to increase until
they exceed her exports, when reaction and depression will
inevitably follow.

The rate of foreign exchange is held to be a matter of
much importance to the business of the country. In itself,
the difference of exchange is a matter of but little moment :—
the extreme variation in time of peace being but two or
three per cent.—the expense of transporting the precious
metals. It is important mainly as an indication of the current of gold and silver, whether to or from our country.
When foreign exchange is high, and continues high, it is an
indication that the current of gold is from our country; and
a contraction of the currency and a depression of prices is
apprehended. When it is low it indicates that the current
of gold is toward this country, or at least, that the current
from our mines to foreign countries is not stimulated by
any extraordinary demand; and consequently a drain of
gold, a contraction of the currency and business depression
are not anticipated. Hence, high rates of exchange were
regarded with dread, while low rates always inspired confidence and hope. The rate of exchange indicates a favorable or unfavorable balance of trade.

I now invite particular attention to a most important fact,
or effect, resulting from an irredeemable currency; a fact
that is clearly understood by but few, even of those who
have made finance a study:

*An irredeemable currrency reverses all the indications of a
favorable or unfavorable balance of trade and of high or low
rates of foreign exchange.*

This is the sphinx of the financial question. The price
of gold—the premium—has become the best indication of

the business prospect. And, contrary to the common opinion, a rise of gold is a favorable indication, and a fall of gold is the reverse.

A rise in the price of gold is found to accompany high rates of foreign exchange. Financiers and business men who have not learned that the indications of foreign exchange have been reversed by an irredeemable currency, continue to regard high rates of foreign exchange as an indication unfavorable to business; and have come to regard its accompanying firmness of, or rise in the price of gold as having the same effect, and, consequently, with foreboding of evil; also, as affecting or reflecting upon the credit of the government. A fall in the price of gold, though really unfavorable to business, is by a large majority of the people regarded as a favorable indication; because, first, it is in the line of resumption, which nearly everybody appears to desire without knowing why; and, second, because it is accompanied by low rates of exchange which still continue to be regarded as a certain indication favorable to business. This continual dependence upon the old guide boards which have been reversed, leads the Resumptionists to set their faces in the wrong direction, and though they realize that it is a "hard road to travel," they are confident that there is "milk and honey" at the end of their journey.

This reversal of the "indications," as before stated, is owing to the precious metals having changed their relations to commerce and business, by being demonetized by an irredeemable currency. Their export now has the same effect as that of any other product and conduces to the prosperity of the country. It does not diminish our currency—it simply tends to raise the price of gold correspondingly with the demand. This demand for and export of gold is to effect an equation of trade. When the demand has effected a rise in the price of gold, it is thereby turned to other exportable products until the increased demand for them raises their price also, when the demand returns again to gold. The importation of gold adds to our domestic supply, depressing its price and thereby attracting the demand for exports to gold and leaving other products until their prices are depressed in sympathy with gold, when again they share the common demand.

With an irredeemable legal-tender currency, *whatever be the magnitude of our imports on the basis of domestic values, our exports must be of an equal or greater magnitude,* or *the difference will be a foreign debt,* to be paid at a future time by exports on the same basis of values.

If our imports for a time exceed our exports the difference is a foreign debt. This debt is in all the various forms of national, state, county, city, and corporation bonds and securities: also in personal and mercantile credits. These latter are usually of comparatively limited amount and of a temporary character, while the former are of great magnitude and of a more permanent character.

Our securities sold abroad have all the relations to commerce of exports. They take the place of exports in effecting for the time being an equation of trade. They are in direct competition with all other exports and depress their prices, and might be classed as exports; and when they return for payment or purchase they should be regarded as imports, as they must then be paid for or equated by exports. But their effect upon business is different from that of any other class of exports or imports, and, for the purpose of considering the effects of their exportation and return upon the prices of exportable commodities and upon business and money distribution, I shall treat them as foreign indebtedness in accordance with the common idea.

What is the magnitude of this foreign indebtedness? It is probably more than two billions; it may be not less than three billions. Whatever is its precise amount it is enormous. The great wonder has been how the country holds up under it and seems to prosper. It is generally predicted that the interest will become unendurable, and that the principal, when demanded, will be our utter ruin; that in that evil day there will be a universal "break-up;" and panic, stagnation, paralysis and bankruptcy will reign supreme. Were we to resume specie payments, and adopt a specie basis, we should *thereby invite these calamities from our foreign indebtedness.*

Our irredeemable legal-tender currency saves us from these evil results.

We are a debtor nation, and shall continue to be, so long as we give a larger per centage of interest and profits on loans and investments than is common in other countries. This is our chronic condition, the end of which no man can see. In view of this fact, our irredeemable legal-tender currency is a blessing—it is the talisman that makes us master of the situation—the shield that saves us from impending danger—the wand that changes a curse to a benefaction. Let us consider how this is:

If we estimate the interest-bearing foreign debt in the form of permanent securities, at two billions, the annual interest as at six per cent., would amount to $120,000,000. The principal is a gold debt, and the interest is a gold current accruing obligation. This latter amounts to about twice the product of our mines. It is a constant demand for our precious metals, and drains our country of them, but it cannot drain from us our currency nor affect its volume. Business is not only not paralyzed by this drain of gold, but, on the contrary, is stimulated and improved by it. Our domestic product of the precious metals only half supplies this demand. If it seeks more it raises their price. This causes it to seek other of our products in our markets as its only alternative, thus finding an outlet and market for our surplus products—while our currency remains within our own country, undisturbed in volume, fulfilling its beneficent purposes: and the effect the payment of this interest has upon general business is to quicken its activities and give firmness to our market prices. Thus of the interest, what of the principal?

The aggregate of our foreign debt will, probably, not be much diminished for a generation to come. It may be increased, but it is not likely to be increased to any considerable extent or so rapidly as it has been in the last decade. Old debts will be paid and new debts created, continuing the aggregate as large or larger than at present. To preserve the aggregate as it is, *our exports must exceed our imports an amount equal to the interest of the indebtedness.* A greater excess of exports will diminish the aggregate; a less excess of exports will increase it.

Our foreign indebtedness may be paid directly by the contracting parties at maturity, or indirectly by American purchases of these securities for investment until they mature. In either case, the general effect upon business will be the same. Suppose a hundred millions should mature or be purchased annually, the effect of their payment would be the same upon business as that of the payment of the interest before illustrated—to quicken into greater activity all our industries by creating a greater demand, and opening a wider outlet and market for all our exportable commodities, giving firmness and buoyancy to all nominal and market prices. Should the amount be two hundred millions, or three hundred millions, the effect would be the same, but greater in degree. Enterprise and industry would be the more stimulated. The increased taxation on the part of the general government, states, counties or cities, rendered necessary to cancel their maturing bonds, would be compensated by the increased activity and buoyancy of business. An increased product of wealth would result from this increased business, activity sufficient to fill the vacancies created by the exportation of commodities to liquidate the matured or purchased indebtedness. Thus the country would exert a little more energy and muscle, but would be no poorer during or after the payment than before.

While we retain our legal tender currency, certain commercial contingencies that may arise would have a very different effect upon our business prosperity from that which would be experienced if we resume specie payments. Should there be a serious commercial crisis in England or Germany, the holders of our securities might wish to turn them into money as soon as possible to relieve their pressing necessities. In such a case, two or three or four hundred millions, more or less, might suddenly be returned and placed upon our markets to be sold for what they would bring. The placing of large quantities upon our market would reduce their price (in our market) by their superabundance. When they had been sold at a discount for currency, this currency must be converted into gold or other commodities, which from this excessive demand would rise in price. Thus we should buy our securities at a discount, and pay for them with domestic products at a premium. *This would be buying cheap and selling dear*—reversing the condition under specie payments.

While we retain our currency we are strong in our international relations. The shrewd leaders of public opinion in foreign countries will be wary how they create a panic among their people against our credit or our securities by warlike menace or otherwise. Their interests are on the side of peace and fair dealing. If they depreciate our securities and throw them back upon us for redemption before maturity, their own people only will have their fingers burnt. We can stand it if they can. How much of our success may have been due to these considerations in our past negotiations! Why should we surrender this masterly position?

Resumption of specie payments would reverse all these conditions. To pay the annual interest would drain us of the precious metals. The basis of the currency—gold and silver—having been drawn from us, the currency resting upon it must suffer contraction until the prices of our exports could find a profitable market abroad. Low nominal values would probably be a chronic condition. I say probably, because high nominal values might be maintained. by enacting a sufficiently high tariff. But if we have not the sagacity to see the disadvantages of resumption, we may not have the sagacity to see the advantages of a high tariff under resumption. A prevalence of low prices would relatively augment our indebtedness. A financial panic in England or Germany would bring upon us universal bankruptcy—in several ways. Business being paralyzed there, the principal market of our leading exports would be virtually closed; at the same time payment would be demanded for all our matured and mercantile foreign indebtedness, and our unmatured securities would be returned to our markets. All these causes would contribute to rapidly contract our currency and shrink our nominal values. All business would be blocked and general bankruptcy would be inevitable. With specie payments the remotest hamlet in the far west would be directly affected by every movement of the bankers of the great commercial cities of western Europe. If the Bank of England should raise its rate of interest as it did last year, in the course of a few months, from three to seven per cent., it would seriously and detrimentally affect business and the prices of products—especially exportable products — all over our country. The Bank of England could depress our markets, just when we have crops to sell, by raising the rates of exchange against us, and by raising her rates of interest and curtailing her loans — creating a temporary tightness or scarcity of money and alarm until our products could be purchased at low prices, when she could lower her interest and extend her loans — reviving confidence and leading to an extension of credit to our importing merchants (mostly foreign agents), who in turn would extend credits to our purchasers, who would thus be induced to purchase imports on a rising market until our crops were ready to move forward again, when the process would be repeated.

With specie payments the burden of finding gold to make foreign payments is upon us, and if too scarce at home it must be sought abroad under any or every adverse circumstance. In all gold-base currency countries gold becomes periodically too scarce to make the necessary payments to balance accounts, when it must be sought abroad under great sacrifices. All nations, at such times, are dependent and harassed. And a nation like ours, that is constantly in debt to foreign countries, is constantly dependent upon the monetary condition of those countries that hold its maturing and interest-bearing securities—and is largely dependent upon their forbearance and good will.

With specie payments an enemy might injure us seriously simply by a menace of war, which would have the effect of returning to our markets our foreign securities in such volume as to suddenly drain away our precious metals, leading to a sudden contraction of our currency—a shrinkage of prices and panic. If severe, the government itself might be forced to suspend its guaranty of specie redemption of a bond-secured gold-note currency. In such a state of things, the only currency in the hands of the people would pass at a discount, not being a legal-tender. The government might refuse, for taxes, the currency it had guaranteed—or it might accept it at par, and disburse it at a discount; and, to make up the deficiency, levy more taxes, or resort to more loans. Such periods germinate to seeds of repudiation, discontent and anarchy.

To recapitulate, we have shown that resumption is delusive—that though it exists with prosperity, it is not only no guaranty against, but is necessarily followed by adversity. That it necessarily involves expansion and contraction of the currency. That this is the case whether we have the old State banks, the old U. S. Bank System, or a pure metallic currency, or a bond-secured gold-note currency. That it involves necessarily an unfavorable balance of trade by imports *at high prices* to be equated only through an excess of exports *at low prices*, causing us to buy dear and sell cheap—that these results are inseparable from a gold-base currency. That it would make our foreign indebtedness a chronic burden, and an instrumentality of periodical oppression, and at all times a menace in the hands of foreign nations to humble our national pride, and to control our diplomacy; that by making our currency in unison with that of foreign countries, and placing our business on the same basis, we should surrender the monetary independence we now have, and place our business prosperity in irretreivable subjection to the contingencies or machinations which control or direct the monetary conditions and movements of the great money center of the world—London—Lombard street, and the Bank of England. That, on the contrary, our irredeemable legal-tender currency—being subject to law, enables the government to determine its quantity at all times, and to issue it, and continue it in a fixed ratio to the population using it—establishing a uniform amount per capita—thus establishing a more steady and uniform measure of nominal values of long duration, beyond the term of ordinary contracts, than is possible with a metallic or gold currency. That it enables us to purchase our imports and sell our exports at our own market prices, measured by a uniform currency.

That it effects an equation of trade with foreign countries, without affecting the volume of our currency, or disturbing unfavorably our market prices. That it renders us, in a great measure, independent of the monetary conditions of other nations. That it subjects the precious metals, like all other commodities, to the law of demand and supply. That it renders our foreign indebtedness easy to be borne, by enabling us to pay, both interest and principal, in domestic products, at our market prices, and not in currency, thus leaving our currency undiminished in volume, to preserve the measure of values unaffected except by the demand for our products; and that it utterly disables any, or all, foreign nations from injuring our interests, or business prosperity, or limiting our independence, or humbling our pride by any vindictive attempt to depress our national or international credit.

I have said that, with our irredeemable currency, whatever be the magnitude of our imports on the basis of domestic values, *our exports must be of an equal magnitude on the same basis of value,* or the difference will be a foreign debt *to be paid by exports* on the basis of domestic values.

I wish to further consider this proposition, partly to better define my meaning, but more particularly to draw attention to the manner in which this principle affects business prosperity, and the extent of its influence. When I affirm that our imports and exports are based upon domestic prices, I am not to be understood to affirm that, they bear no relation to foreign prices, or that they are unaffected by foreign prices. There is always a direct relation between domestic and foreign prices through the medium of the gold premium. And the state of foreign markets, as prices in them rise or fall, affects directly the domestic price of all exportable commodities, and that of many, if not all of our imports. My endeavor is to contrast the conditions under which our imports are purchased and exports sold in our markets with an irredeemable currency, with those under which imports are purchased and exports sold with a gold, or gold-base paper currency. With an irredeemable currency, if our market prices are inflated the premium on gold is the measure of that inflation; and the foreign merchant, when he sells his goods at our inflated prices, must rebate a percentage of those prices in proportion to the inflation when he converts his currency into gold by suffering the loss of the difference between gold and currency, if he take away his pay in gold. If he chooses to take some other of our exportable commodities, he finds them ranging at prices, nominally higher, perhaps, then in the country to which he wishes to take them. But, as he must rebate his currency to convert it into gold, he has only to rebate our currency prices of other commodities in the same ratio, to convert them into gold prices, from which he determines whether he will buy gold or some other exportable commodity, or a bill of exchange. Thus our currency prices, for the purposes of commerce, are converted into gold by the rebate of the gold premium.

The excess of imports over exports, less the interest on the foreign indebtedness, is equal to the augmentation of foreign indebtedness.

The effects of the increase of foreign indebtedness are very different under an irredeemable legal tender currency from those under a gold-base currency. This difference has its peculiar effects upon commerce, the gold premium, the relative prices of different classes of domestic products, and upon different sections and pursuits.

The great excess of imports over exports during the last decade is owing to the great increase of our foreign indebtedness.

Perhaps the reader will say I have taken the effect for the cause. Let us see.

During the rebellion nearly all our national bonds were taken by our own people; also, to a great extent, our railroad bonds of roads constructed since the commencement of the war, and probably not less than eighty or ninety per cent. of all our securities, national, State, county, city and corporation, issued during the war, remained in domestic hands at its close. Where are they now? Would it be too much to estimate that fifty per cent. of all American securities issued since the commencement of the war, have, since its close, passed to foreign hands? And if not, can the amount be less than $1,500,000,000? Before the war the foreign indebtedness was estimated at more than $500,000,-

000. If we estimate that $500,000,000 were added during the war, and $1,500,000,000 from its close to the close of 1873, we should have an aggregate of $2,500,000,000 as the sum of our foreign indebtedness. For the want of reliable statistics I can only approximate the amount, and according to the reader's information it may be deemed too high or too low, and can be modified accordingly. For the purposes of illustrating the principle in view, I shall assume the aggregate of American Securities placed upon foreign markets during the eight years preceding 1874 as not less than $1,200,000,000.

The exportation of securities enables us to retain our gold by enabling us to draw bills of foreign exchange against them, to pay for our imports; and if we export them in great quantities we shall import gold in payment for them. Gold being the basis of the currency (with specie payments), by being retained as it is produced in our mines, or by being imported, it increases the volume of the currency either by entering directly into circulation, or by being employed as bank reserves on which is issued a still greater increase of the volume of the currency; thus increasing and inflating the currency, and enhancing prices, reviving and quickening business. On the other hand, to pay their annual interest, or the principal at maturity, or their repurchase for investment, is depressing to business, because these deplete the country of its gold, contract the currency, depress prices and obstruct business; and should they be returned to us in great volume, the paralysis of business and monetary distress resulting would be very great.

With an irredeemable currency the exporting of securities has a depressing effect upon business. They become a substitute for gold or other of our exportable products in amount equal to their gold value abroad. They are exported because they are the cheapest, at the time, of all our exports. An importer having imported a quantity of goods and sold them in our markets, has received our irredeemable currency in payment for them. He must convert his currency into some of our exports in order to make his payment where he obtained his imports. If our securities have advanced in foreign markets, or declined in our market relative to other exports, they are sent abroad for sale. This increases the volume of foreign exchange in our market, depressing the price of bills of foreign exchange relatively to the prices of exports. The importer, therefore, finds it to his advantage to buy bills of foreign exchange drawn against securities sold abroad, or to buy securities in our market direct and ship them abroad, rather than buy our gold, cotton, tobacco, wheat, or any other of our exports. ' Thus, so long as our securities find a profitable market abroad, their exportation depresses the price of gold and the price of all other exportable products.

The effect of augmenting our foreign indebtedness by selling our securities in foreign markets is, *first*, to depress the price of gold in common with, and in like manner and degree that it depresses the prices of all other exportable products. Its second effect is to stimulate importation, and thereby to depress the prices of all our domestic products, which come into competition with imported articles. ·

To reduce the premium on gold while our currency prices remain the same, is the same in effect as reducing the tariff.

To illustrate this, let us suppose that an importer sells in our market a yard of cloth for $5.00, currency prices, when gold is selling at 1.25 per cent. Suppose the tariff upon that class of cloth is one dollar a yard in gold. It is but reasonable to suppose that the importer makes a fair profit upon his trade; and we will also suppose that domestic producers in competition with the importer, also sell a like article at $5.00 per yard, at a like reasonable profit. It is evident that the importer must pay $1.25 of currency to obtain his gold dollar to pay the tariff. This leaves him $3.75 currency, for which he can obtain $3.00 in gold, to pay costs of production, transportation and profit.

Now suppose gold to decline to $1.10 per cent. The importer sells a like yard of cloth for $5.00; and the domestic producer also sells a like yard of cloth for $5.00. It is evident that the importer can obtain a gold dollar to pay the tariff for $1.10 currency, leaving him $3.90 currency to be converted into gold, which gives him $3.54, to pay cost of production, transportation and profit.

This is an increase of 18 per cent. over his former gold

3

proceeds. If we suppose his profit under the higher gold rats was 10 per cent., and that he can repeat his importations, or return the same capital twice a year, his profits would be 20 per cent. per annum. His profits having been increased 18 per cent. by the fall of gold, each return of his capital now yields him 28 per cent. or 56 per cent. per annum. It is fair to presume that the domestic producer obtained an annual profit of 20 per cent., equally with the importer, under the higher gold rate, prices being supposed to have adjusted themselves to that rate. So long as the price of the cloth produced and the costs of production remained the same, the producer's profits remained 20 per cent. per annum, while the importer's profits had been increased to 56 per cent. per annum. Is it not evident that importation would be stimulated until the price of cloth became depressed?

During the depression, while the entire margin of profits of the domestic producer would be dwindling to zero, the profits of the importer would be constantly greater than during the higher gold premium. Is it a matter of astonishment, therefore, that New York and Boston importers, and the papers in their interest, and the bankers and capitalists immediately connected and interested with them should be demonstrative to promote legislation to reduce the gold premium to zero, and to provide for an early return to specie payments?

It is seldom that there is a sudden and considerable rise or fall of gold, without its being succeeded by a modifying re-action. The "Gold Ring," or "Gamblers in gold," so called, cannot produce a rise or fall of gold that will not be soon followed by re-action through the laws of trade, and transient undulations have but little general effect upon the business of the country. The average tendency through long periods determines the general effects.

However gradual the decline of the gold premium, though its burdens may be mitigated by some reductions in the costs of production, by greater opportunity to effect this through longer periods of time, they are burdens still upon domestic producing industry, and at length become paralytic to production and business—as in the late panic which was most oppressive at the period when the gold premium was the lowest, and became less oppressive as the gold rate rose from 1.08 to 1.14—yet the leading New York papers that plume themselves upon their superior financial knowledge, repeatedly congratulated the country upon the low gold premium and the "approach" to specie payments—the low rates of foreign exchange, and the return of gold to this country !—which latter was like carrying coals to Newcastle, or importing breadstuffs from Liverpool to New York, in the early part of 1837, at a cost of $10.00 per bbl., only to be re-shipped to Europe during the succeeding summer, on a sale at $5.00 per bbl.

But though the loss to the producer, by a decline of the prices of products, may be mitigated, it is never compensated, because many of the elements of cost are of a fixed character, as interest on capital invested, taxes, insurance, etc., while others are fixed for long periods of time, as leases, contracts, salaries, commissions, transportation, etc., etc. It is a very common and a very grave error, to suppose that contraction and expansion of the currency, affect all prices and costs in like manner, degree and simultaneously. Some are affected primarily, immediately and intensely; others, secondarily, tertiarily, or more remotely, and in a degree modified by their proximity or remoteness in the chain of cause and effect to or from the principal operative cause.

If the decline of the gold rate—fifteen per cent.—be gradual, and distributed over a period of two or three years, it may be borne with a fair degree of prosperity. Though the anticipated profits fail to be realized, something will be gained; and business will continue to move in its accustomed channels, though not with its accustomed alertness and buoyancy; but if a similar permanent decline occur in a single year, its depressing effects could not fail to be serious and embarrassing.

Our securities sold abroad, have depressed the price of gold and the prices of all exportable products, and directly stimulated and largely augmented importations, and repressed and diminished exportations. Therefore, the augmentation of foreign indebtedness has caused the great excess of imports over exports.

The mal-policy, therefore, of unnecessarily issuing bonds to be floated to foreign markets, is not unlike grappling Productive Industry by the throat, to afford an opportunity to foreigners to rifle his pockets.

Let us now consider the effects of the augmentation of foreign indebtedness upon the distribution of the currency. It is claimed and conceded, that the west and south have too little money in proportion to their business wants relative to the north and east, and a remedy is sought in the establishment of more banks in those sections. They are entitled to their proportion if they want them, I refrain, however, from discussing this remedy; I cite it as showing the scarcity of money in those sections. Senator Schurz has said that the remedy is fallacious, and that what is really needed in the south and west is more capital. This, if true, is too vague to be understood—capital is not necessarily money; and what is asked for is more money. I suppose he would call the cotton crop capital. But an increase of the crop twenty-five per cent. might have impoverished instead of enriching the south. It would involve greater cost of production, preparation and transportation; while its increased volume might depress its price in a proportionate ratio, yielding less net proceeds than the late crop.

If we suppose that the sale abroad of our securities, has had the effect to keep the average premium on gold twenty per cent below what it would have been, had there been no increase of our foreign indebtedness, we may form an estimate of the effect this fact would have upon the distribution of currency. Taking the present gold rate at $1.15, we estimate (for illustration) the value of the principal staples exported from the Southern States proper, including that which is consumed within our country outside of the Southern States, and including costs of transportation and freight to a foreign market of that which is shipped abroad, as not less than $400,000,000, at the foreign gold valuation. This, converted into currency, would be $460,000,000. This is the amount of currency those States would be entitled to draw within their borders during the season. (Their wants and supplies would probably return it all—I am not considering that point—and, in fact, the currency itself might never pass either way—bills of inland exchange taking its place to a great extent.) If the gold rate were twenty per cent. higher—1.35—the gold value of her exports would be convertible into $540,000,000 of currency, enabling the Southern States to draw to themselves $80,000,000 more currency by her annual exports than they are enabled to draw under the low gold rate of 1.15, thus increasing her receipts from her surplus products more than seventeen per cent.

This increased volume of receipts would be the increased value of the exports of the South, and would give rise to an increased value of imports to supply her wants. It would not be a clear gain to her to this amount, as many of her supplies would be enhanced in cost to her by the same cause—the higher premium on gold; but she would gain more than she would lose—the magnitude of her commerce with her sister States would be increased. She would have more money to do business with, and prices and values of all kinds would be favorably affected, and all business within her borders would be very much revived thereby.

If the Western and South-western States send eastward for export and for consumption in the Atlantic States an amount double that estimated as sent from the South, we have a gold value of $800,000,000. This at the present rate of gold is convertible into $920,000,000 currency. Were the gold rate 1.35 instead of 1.15—as it is assumed it would be, were it not for the export of securities—the western exports of $800,000.000, gold value, would be convertible into $1,080,000,000—a difference in her favor from the same surplus products of $160,000,000 currency—over 17 per cent. added to the value of her exports. Thus would the Western States be enabled to draw to themselves, through their annual exports on the present basis of production and consumption, $160,000,000 more currency, or currency values in bills of inland exchange, than they can control under the present low gold rate. This would give great relief to their depressed industry and business.

If it be thought the above estimates are too high, either of the depression of the gold rate from the cause named, or the aggregate shipments from the South and West, a very large reduction may be made from the aggregate result—a reduction of three-eighths—and still leave an increase of currency to the South of $50,000,000, and to the West of $100,000,000—an increase of nearly eleven per cent. over their present receipts from their surplus products.

If the cause of this difference in the gold rate—the increase of our foreign indebtedness—has become inoperative, from the exhaustion of foreign credit, or from the exhaustion of our securities available to send abroad—or if, from any cause, our foreign indebtedness shall not increase at a rate greater than the sum of the interest of that indebtedness—then we have arrived at conditions under which our imports cannot exceed our exports. Also, it is quite probable, if our present legal tender irredeemable currency shall be maintained, that in the ten years succeeding the 1st of January, 1874, our exports (including the precious metals) will exceed our imports in currency values at least one billion dollars. The conditions and results of our foreign commerce will be very different and very much subject to oscillations if steps be taken and persisted in to return to a system of specie payments.

Were the volume of the currency to be enlarged definitely in the ratio of the increase of population, the South and West would enjoy the full measure of the benefit of the changed conditions of commerce. The gold rate would rise and the increased currency values would be at least 10 per cent. for the same quantities of products exported from those sections.

How would this affect the Eastern and Northern States. They are enabled to be consumers of Southern and Western products in a great measure, because the South and West consume their products. The market for their products in the South and West, will be enlarged in the ratio of the increased prosperity of those sections. Even if the quantities of goods transported either way, between the sections named were no greater, their values would be increased 10 per cent., because, as has been shown, the South and West would have 10 per cent. more money to spend annually, and it would return in the same time to the East and North for supplies. Add to this, that a prosperous people always produce more and consume more, and we may reasonably infer that the internal commerce would be increased in magnitude in the increased quantity of products exchanged as well as in increased nominal values.

The products of the North and East would be enhanced in value, equally with those of the South and West, though not simultaneously. The South and West producing more largely of exportable products, whose price is greatly dependent upon the foreign market price, the demand for which would be directly increased, by an increase of the gold rate, their prices would be most immediately affected; while the prices of Eastern and Northern products, mainly depending upon domestic markets, and affected by the competition of foreign importations, would be affected indirectly by the rise of the gold rate, which would repress importations like an additional tariff, until the market prices of those products should rise proportionatly to the increase of the gold rate; also would they be affected by the increased demand from the South and West, at least an increase of a hundred and fifty millions annually. Thus would the prosperity of one section react upon, and inspire that of the other.

In supposing the gold rate to rise above its present range, I have coupled it with the condition that the volume of currency be increased correspondingly with the increase of population. This would be the best policy to pursue, but it is probable we shall have no increase of the currency. What, then, will be the probable effect with a fixed quantity of currency, limited, for all purposes to $756,000,000. This contemplates the withdrawal of the $26,000,000—of the reserve already issued, contracting the present volume in circulation to that amount directly; and by the growth of population is an indirect contraction, and both tend to reduce the gold premium.

The cessation of the increase of foreign indebtedness will have a contrary effect. This cause may be sufficiently powerful to more than counteract the effect of contraction. We may see therefore an apparent paradox of a rising gold

premium, in the face of an actual contraction and an in-
verse contraction by the growth of population. But if the
gold rate do not rise, and hold a higher range with some
degree of steadiness, the cause cited will prevent its rapid
decline, and it probably stands higher now than it would
have done at this time, if we had not met a check in placing our railroad and other securities upon a foreign market.
If gold should rise, the effect upon the money distribution
would be as stated; first, enabling the South and West to
draw to themselves a larger proportion of the whole volume
in circulation. The North and East would have less than
they have had. The South and West affording a better
market for many of the products of the North and East,
would enable those industries producing those products,
and industries most nearly related thereto, to draw to themselves such a portion of the common currency, as is necessary to their prosecution to the extent of supplying the
demand. Upon this hypothesis it is evident that the South
and West, and the active producing industries of the North
and East, will draw to themselves a larger proportion of the
common fund of the national currency. This involves the
corollary that some localities or pursuits, will draw to themselves a less porportion of the common stock of currency,
than they have been able to during the period of the exportation of our securities. This effect will not be felt by
localities or sections, as it will be by pursuits.

It has been charged against our irredeemable currency,
as inhering to it, and inseparable from it; that it flooded our
markets with excessive importations; that it encouraged
reckless speculation in stocks; and that it gave fictitious values, and led to over speculation generally, and especially in
real estate. Our excessive importations cannot be continued; they will probably fall short in the five years from the
first of January, 1874, more than $500,000,000 of what they
were in the five years preceding. The money required to
move these imports in our markets will be released from
this service, and will flow into the south and west, whither
it will be drawn as has been set forth, and to the producing
industries of the north and east.

The productive industries and pursuits having become

more powerful to draw a larger proportion of the whole volume of currency into their service, either by enhanced prices of products, or by holding the same prices in the face of an expanding population with a fixed volume of currency, other pursuits adversely affected, or affected favorably in a less degree, must relinquish a portion of the currency they have heretofore drawn to their service and control. For this reason it may reasonably be anticipated that a much less proportion can flow into the service of stock speculation. The tendency has been for money to *flow* into that service because the productive industries, having been depressed, were less inviting or perhaps repellant to enterprise and investment; which were turned to more inviting pursuits, the principle of which was speculation in stocks and real estate. But these pursuits will not be seriously or improperly affected; they will be relieved, however, of the temptations of vast quantities of unemployed capital seeking investment. With a growing population profitably employed in all its industrial activities, real estate is guaranteed sustained, or ascending prices, and the increased and increasing internal commerce of the country cannot fail to yield fair returns to all legitimate and properly conducted transportation investments; and their quoted prices will depend more upon such returns, and less upon Wall street manipulation, while fancy stocks will find less reservoirs of money to float upon.

Many of the phenomena of business, prices and commerce presented as "*the* inseparable *evils* of a paper currency" are caused by the exportation of our securities. To illustrate this, and for further comment, I introduce the following extract from a late speech of Senator Jones of Nevada, in the U. S. Senate:

"If money is scarce, I ask in the name of common sense, why will not people give more for it? Why do not the values of property in this country bear some just relation to the values of property all over the world? Why, sir, the premium on gold does not fully show the depreciation of this paper; and there is the difficulty. I differed from nearly every Senator on this floor in the reasons which induced me to support the amendment introduced by the Senator from New Jersey; [Mr. Frelinghuysen.] Objection was made by friends of that amendment that it would have a tendency to make gold rise in price. Now, sir, I say gold ought to rise. Every other commodity in this country—butchers' meat, groceries, provisions and everything that enters into domestic use has risen, so that in relation to them greenbacks are really at a depreciation of fully forty per cent. while in relation to gold, which has been shorn of its chief uses by being demonetized, the same greenbacks are at a depreciation of only ten or twelve per cent. The effect of this is to discourage mining enterprises and depress mining interests, If the Government ever intends to resume specie payments those interests should be stimulated and encouraged by every legitimate means.

"There is no demand for gold in this country beyond the small amount necessary to pay the duties on imports and the interest on the national debt. When I come here from Nevada with gold and silver—the only money in circulation there—and find that it is too low in price, I cannot help it. In order to get its full value I must engage in foreign trade, become a gambler in the gold-room, or leave this country and go to France, England, or some other country where gold is the standard and circulates at its full value. If I stay here I must trade it for paper at a premium of from ten to twelve per cent. which, as I said before, is much less than the difference between paper and every other commodity. I have no remedy. I must submit to the loss. It is to the interest of this country that the real depreciation of paper should be exactly measured by the premium on gold. That this is not the case there are examples all around us to prove. That no good does or can result from this state of things can be easily demonstrated. For example, suppose 1,000 wagons can be made in this country at $100 apiece; as gold stands now the foreigner who would like to purchase them and thus give us an export trade to balance off some of our imports could pay for them with $90,000. But he can get them for $85,000 in a country where gold circulates as money and this country loses the business. Now suppose gold should go up to 1.25, where it really belongs, in that case he could pay for the same wagons with $80,000 in gold, and still not disturb the relation between paper and anything else in the country. This would make possible an export trade that is not possible now, owing to the depreciation of gold. In other words, gold is the cheapest thing in this country, and the commodities sent here from every portion of the earth seek that in exchange in preference to anything else we produce. We can export nothing so readily as gold. It is the cheapest commodity we have, and it is, therefore, in the greatest demand for exportation."

The principle point in the foregoing is, that the gold premium is too low to measure the true difference between the currency prices of many articles, and what he assumes as the true gold price, judging from ante-war prices. The only cause he assigns for this difference is, that gold has been demonetized, and, consequently, not wanted for the purposes of money.

Before gold was demonetized there was no premium. A gold premium presupposes the demonetization of gold. How, then, can the simple demonetization depress the premium? If gold shall be re-monetized the premium will disappear altogether. How, then, can a high premium on gold be preserved by making gold the monetary base? Perhaps Mr. Jones would have expressed his idea better if he had said the premium on gold of late years has given to gold a less purchasing power in our markets than it would have had if gold were the monetary base. Also, we infer his meaning to be, that if the Government had hoarded gold to the amount of $250,000,000—an amount proportionate to the whole amount of currency, equal to the ante-war bank reserves—that this quantity would be withdrawn thereby from the gold supply for exportation, and by diminishing the supply would raise the gold premium. This would have been the effect. But it would only have counteracted one fourth of the adverse effect resulting from the exportation during the same period of $1,000,000,000 of securities. Had the Government hoarded $250,000,000, over its present hoards, there would be outstanding an equal amount of six per cent. bonds which have been purchased and canceled. Such hoarding, therefore, would cost, on interest account, $15,000,000 annually.

Previous to those bonds being purchased and canceled, they were afloat and seeking a market, and had they not been purchased by the Government they would probably have gone abroad, *and been added* to the volume of our exported securities. In that case their effect upon the gold premium would have exactly balanced and canceled the effect of the hoarding of the gold, and the Government would have lost $15,000,000 annual interest, without any compensation therefor to the people.

The less purchasing power of gold of late years results primarily and mainly from the great increase of our foreign indebtedness, in connection with another and secondary cause, before alluded to—that of the different effects upon different classes of commodities and forms of wealth, in time and degree, as, in their relations, they are near to, or remote from, the active cause. Gold and all exportable products are first affected; products (including manufactures) in competition with imports are subsequently affected indirectly and to a less degree by the increased facilities for importation, resulting from a low gold premium; while those products or pursuits and forms of wealth which are little affected by the conditions of foreign commerce are last and least affected, as buildings and building material, transportation investments, real estate—rents, leases—contracts extending over long periods of time—salaries for long terms, national, State, and municipal expenses involving taxation, and transportation expenses, etc. These have an innate power of resistance to declining prices, and form a class of nearly fixed prices, and involve nearly fixed costs to all of those who are under the necessity of paying for their use or appropriation. The prices of the first class have great flexibility; of the second class, less flexibility. This flexibility of prices possessed by the first and second classes has caused those classes to bear a double burden during the decline of gold since the close of the war.

Soon after the close of the war several issues were withdrawn which had served as currency to some extent, as certificates of indebtedness, five per cent. legal tender notes, and compound interest notes. Apart from the withdrawal of these, there has been a direct contraction of the currency, first, by the withdrawal of the reserves, $44,000,000; second, by wastage, which at one quarter of one per cent. per annum of the whole volume for eight years would amount to $15,000,000 (and this is probably too low an estimate), aggregating $59,000,000; and inversely by the growth of population (after spreading the currency over the Southern States, which, though important, I disregard,) in the last eight years, from about $35,000,000 to more than $40,000,000—about fifteen per cent. The burden of this contraction falls mostly or wholly upon those industries producing products of the most flexible prices, because the class of fixed prices tenaciously draws to its own service as large a volume of the common currency as is necessary for its purposes, and the classes of flexible prices must relinquish that amount from their service.

To illustrate: Suppose an agriculturist, as a direct effect of the contractions referred to, finds that his annual products, the same in quantity, bring him two and a half per cent. gross less than the year previous. He finds half his receipts are absorbed in fixed costs of production—such as interest on capital invested or mortgage loans, taxes, insurance, average casualties and accidents, transportation, leases or rents, etc. All these costs remain the same without abatement, and draw to themselves from his gross proceed money sufficient for their payment. His loss by depreciation of prices falls wholly upon the remaining purposes of his proceeds—the payment of his own and his family's labors and the active capital necessary for the next year's operations, being a diminution of five per cent. for these purposes. This continued for a series of years at length becomes burdensome and unbearable, and naturally gives rise to complaints against the government that imposes taxes, middlemen that impose commissions, capitalists that furnish loans, and those who charge the expenses of transportation. It is evident that the agriculturist, from contraction, through the greater flexibility of the proceeds of his products, has become unable to draw to his service so large a proportion of the common currency by a difference of two and a half per cent. of his gross proceeds, and this repeated year after year impoverishes him. Money becomes too scarce with him; and as with him so with whole sections of our country engaged in the same or kindred pursuits. These not only bear their own proper average proportion of the burden of contraction, but have to bear the greater portion of that which should fall to other pursuits and interests, because these latter possess greater power of resistance to any diminution of their income. This principle, in conjunction with the increase of foreign indebtedness, and not the demonetization of gold, causes the relatively low prices of exportable products, including gold.

I agree with Mr. Jones that, "It is the interest of this country that the real depreciation of paper should be exactly measured by the premium on gold;" and "That this is not the case there are examples all around us to prove;" and "That no good does or can result from this state of things." And that many of our manufactures and agricultural products, which at their present currency prices cannot be exported at a profit, if the gold premium were raised sufficiently to measure the true average difference between gold and paper prices, could bear still higher currency

prices and yet be sold in foreign markets for gold at their prices, which, when converted into a quantity of currency corresponding with our increased gold premium would pay remunerative profits to their producers; and this would remove the fallacious objection to our irredeemable currency often presented, that it has closed foreign markets to many of our manufactures by having raised the currency cost of production out of proportion to the foreign gold price.

To give the gold premium this property of exactly or approximately measuring the average difference between gold and paper prices, and to remove by abolishing (not by readjusting) burdens which are now unequally borne, there should be a limited enlargement of the volume of the currency, and thereafter a constant enlargement of the quantity of the currency in the ratio of the increase of the population using it, and a cessation of the enlargement of our foreign indebtedness. To promote the latter let statesmen be wary how they multiply bonds to be exported to foreign markets. If bonds must be issued, it is policy to induce them to stay at home; and to this end let them be explicitly payable, principal and interest, in currency, and then the less issued the better.

The public mind has been and still continues to be infatuated with the idea that it is desirable to bring the current or convertible value of the currency dollar and gold dollar to par with each other. This is a mischievous and costly infatuation, tending directly to malpolicy and adversely to the country's prosperity. The two kinds of dollars are distinctly different, and there is no reason whatever why they should be of the same current or convertible value.

It were just as sensible to insist that two kinds of grain should always be of the same convertible value, or cotton and wool, or any other two commodities that may accidentally be of the same price betimes.

The aggregate of prices and specific prices of all exchangeable commodities and values become adjusted through the laws of trade, to the aggregate of legal tender currency and currency convertible into legal tender at par (bank currency) in active circulation, in the same manner that prices adjust themselves to all currencies, at all periods and in all countries. Thus our national currency becomes the measure of values or prices, and has itself a corresponding current, convertible, legal tender par value: in the same manner as have all legal tender currencies and currencies convertible into legal tender at par, as was the case with gold and silver and bank currency before the war. (And even when the practical currency is not legal tender, and ceases to be convertible into legal tender, the quantity in circulation, deducting the discount by depreciation, continues to measure prices, as was the case with the bank currency during suspension in 1837 and 1857.) Gold, like every other commodity, seeks and finds its own currency price, through the laws of trade; and there is no more reason why a given weight of gold—the gold dollar—should always have the same currency price, than that any other article of commerce should always have the same currency price. Nor is it undesirable that gold should leave our country. It is a product of our mining industry, and it is as advantageous to exchange it in the marts of commerce for other commodities, as to exchange any other product of our industries. In the progress of financial science with us, it has become unnecessary as money; we do not need it. Other nations less progressed do need it; let them have it. As well might the miner miserly hoard it and refuse to part with it for necessaries, conveniences and luxuries, as for us as a nation to refuse, or dread, to part with it to other nations for the same purposes.

Senator Jones perceives and affirms that the gold premium is not the true measure of the difference between gold prices and currency prices. Resumptionists generally endorse and laud this speech. Do they endorse this part of it?

Amasa Walker, in the Overland Monthly for June, 1873, in unison with Mr. Jones, recognizes this fact during the decline of gold, while both are silent in reference to it during the rise of the gold premium. Sam. R. Reed, in The Atlantic Monthly for May, 1873, recognizes this fact both in the rise of the gold premium during the war and its decline and rise at different periods since the war; that during the war, depreciation of the general purchasing power

of the greenback was not nearly so great as that indicated
by the gold premium, and the rapid and great decline of
gold immediately subsequent to the war, was no measure
of the appreciation of the purchasing power of the greenback. Here is the testimony of resumptionists to a general and demonstrable fact, which is ignored by a great
majority of resumptionists, who persistently insist that the
currency fluctuates in value, and the values of all property
and commodities also fluctuate in the exact ratio, and with
every variation of the gold premium. So infatuated are they
with the idea of the necessity of a gold standard of value,
that if by some inconceivable mischance, gold should be
stricken from existence, or transmuted into a baser metal,
they would be at an utter loss to determine whether worldly
wealth thereafter would possess any value whatever. And
so near such a catastrophe is our nation, with only about a
hundred millions left, and that going away at the rate of
over two millions a week, while our product is not more
than half that quantity, that the N. Y. Tribune, in a
paroxysm of alarm, deems it neccessary from its high
pedestal to issue its mandate to the country, to "*Stop that
gold!*"

While the authorities referred to recognize the fact, that
the gold premium does not indicate the purchasing power
of currency, they all three attribute the difference during
the declining phase, to causes immeasurably out of proportion to the effect. Mr. Jones attributes it to the demonetiz-
ing of gold, while the two latter attribute it to the bearing
of the gold market by the Secretary of the Treasury. How
incomparably inadequate these causes appear when compared with the great volume of our securities pressing for a
market, in direct competition with gold and other exports.

Mr. Jones says: "There is no demand for gold in this
country, beyond the small amount necessary to pay the
duties on imports, and the interest on the national debt."
Also in the same paragraph he says: "We can export nothing so readily as gold. It is the cheapest commodity we
have, and it is therefore in the greatest demand for exportation." The logic and consistency (if there be any) in these
sentences are not sufficient to win very enthusiastic admira-

tion. If the demand for gold be the greatest of that of all our exports, how came it to remain constantly the cheapest, while it is at the same time the easiest to export? Has it not yet had time to find its equipoise with other exports? Is it cheaper to export than our securities? Then how comes it that such vast quantities of these are exported, while any gold remains to be had at a cheaper market price? How comes it, if gold is the cheapest and always in greatest demand, that our exports of cotton exceed our gold exports from three to five hundred per cent.?

Mr. Jones speaks of the demand for gold to pay duties on imports *and* the interest on the national debt, as though these were two distinct *demands* upon the market gold supply. The payment of the interest of the national debt, instead of being a demand for gold, furnishes a supply of gold to the market in the same manner that a sale of gold does, and in these two ways the government returns to the market the same quantity that it withdraws from the market by its duties on imports, unless it hoard gold, when it returns a less quantity, and when selling its hoards of gold it supplies a greater quantity than it demands. When a quantity of gold sufficient to fill the channels of this circuit is once appropriated to this purpose, the demand is balanced by the return supply, and both may be disregarded, except so far as the amount necessary for this purpose, or the hoard of gold, be increased or diminished from time to time. Hence, except under the policy of hoarding gold, the only substantial demand for gold is for exportation, in common with all other exportable products, to pay for foreign imports, and to pay our foreign obligations, and the small quantity used in the arts.

He further says: "Gold is the articulation of commerce; it is the most potent agency of civilization. It is gold that has lifted the nations from barbarism." Christianity, science, learning, liberty, law, patriotism, constitutional government, a free press, common education, discovery and invention, one and all, you are "remanded to back seats;" gold comes to the front! Behold and reverence the sovereign that has done what you have so long been credited with doing. Well, well! What next?

4

Mr. Jones further says: "The money, which consists of paper promises, cannot be a standard of value." Supposing that he means to include the legal-tender quality and the general acquiescence of the people in the use of such money, as a currency, I do not hesitate to meet that assertion with one equally emphatic—that it is absolutely false, or, more mildly, a pure fallacy. The experience of the past twelve years proves it a fallacy. Almost every other portion of the speech, from which it is quoted, proves it a fallacy. It is against all past experience of the power of paper currency to measure values. In 1836 and 1856 the bank paper in circulation was the real and active measure of value; while the gold in the bank vaults, on which it purported to be based, and which it purported to represent, but did not, because it was not limited to the same quantity, forming no part of the circulation, had no influence whatever in measuring values. The attempt to bring the paper circulation into correspondence with its assumed base in 1837 and 1857, by contracting the volume of paper, *contracted its measure of values*, and so disturbed the relation between the values of commodities under the new contracted measure of values, and the value of accounts and obligations assumed under the expanded measure of values, that a paralysis of business and general bankruptcy were inevitable. In an article in the *North American Review*, for January, 1874, containing some truths and sound reasoning, with many fallacies, leading to erroneous conclusions, Henry V. Poor recognizes the fact, that our currency measures values by asking: "Why cannot the government now retire its outstanding notes?" and answering: "Because the business of the country has adjusted itself to their present amount." And indeed, all that is said about the rise of prices as the result of inflation, is an acknowledgement that the currency measures values, and is, therefore, the standard of values.

Again: "No government, no people, can be prosperous that ignores the proposition that honesty is the best policy; that by any sort of legislation disturbs the relationship between debtor and creditor." This is very sweeping, certainly. How does it harmonize with bankrupt laws, statutes of limitation, and homesteads and other exemptions from execution? And how does it harmonize with a refusal to legislate to prevent a steady and oppressive contraction which disturbs the relation of debtor and creditor?

Mr. Jones, speaking of California and Nevada, says: "We have never had any money panics. We have never called upon the Congress of the United States to relieve the gambler from any portion of his liabilities, or to issue more money, in order that he might more easily pay his debts."
* * * And closes his speech as follows:

"Gentlemen ask, 'How will you get the gold with which to resume spe-cie payments?' As a general proposition, I would say that the Govern-ment should hoard gold; that it should take no part in the gold gambling of this country. I admit it would be a great injustice to the debtor to say that specie payments shall be resumed immediately, because he contracted his debt when currency was worth about what it is to-day, and it would not be just to make him pay in an appreciated currency. But he has to pay some time. I would put it off three years, and say that on the first day of Jan-uary, or the first day of July, 1877, the greenbacks, the national legal tender, should be redeemed, either in bonds or in gold, at the option of the govern-ment, and destroyed, and at the same time I would repeal the legal tender clause as to all debts contracted after that time. This would be contraction, and would cause a reduction in the price of everything. Without such con-traction the maintenance of the specie standard would be impossible. The effect of that would be to make the condition precedent to a return to specie payments. Unless we make these conditions precedent, unless we fix that time certain in the future, the people will never commence to prepare for it, and will never be more ready than they are to-day."

What does Mr. Jones call a money panic? The failure of the leading banking houses in San Francisco in 1855, and the general depression of business and depreciation of prop-erty in other parts of the State, as well as in San Francisco, was felt with as much severity and was of much longer con-tinuance than the late panic in the currency States. If that was not a money panic we have not had any. A great deal is in a name.

The Hon. Senator says that California and Nevada have never called upon Congress "to relieve the gambler from any portion of his liabilities, or to issue more money, in order that he might the more easily pay his debts." This sentence is worthy of consideration in several respects. The word "gambler" is used to designate those in whose inter-est an enlargement of the volume of currency is assumed to be proposed. The whole tenor of the speech from which I have quoted, shows that the great agricultural industries, and those great sections of our country devoted to them, constituting more than half the territory and fully half the population of the country, have been seriously depressed for many years, and if they seek relief from their unequal burdens, are they to be characterized by opprobrious epithets? These have nothing to do with the laws of trade, and ought to have but little place in statesmanship. But the leading idea is, that the States referred to, have never called upon Congress to legislate upon the finances of the country with a view to their especial benefit. They are modest States, and would not ask for special favors. But then, the Hon. Senator, representing one of those States, before he resumes his seat, recommends that the government should hoard gold as a condition precedent to resumption. This would withdraw from the gold supply two, three, or four hundred millions of dollars, and thereby raise the price of gold. In view of the fact that Nevada is largely engaged in mining the precious metals, the ungenerous may suppose that the principal object in view is to benefit the mining interest, but this can be only incidental to the great national consideration of securing a sound currency. The Senator will, undoubtedly, exercise a christian charity toward his ungenerous critics, when he reflects how he might view a proposition from the South to hoard cotton, her peculiar product, to the value of two, three, or four hundred millions dollars—to withdraw it from the market supply—to raise the market price, and thereafter make it the basis of a circulating medium that it might not return upon the market. Or a similar proposition from the West to hoard wheat or corn; or from Pennsylvania to hoard coal. If these propositions appear very different from the proposition of Mr. Jones, the difference is one of con-sociation or dis-sociation of ideas, more than of principle or philosophy. He does not say how much gold he would hoard, but much or little, the cost of this first step toward resumption would be at least the annual interest of the sum hoarded.

His second proposition is "that on the first day of January, or the first day of July, 1877, the greenbacks, the national legal tenders, should be redeemed, either in bonds or gold, at the option of the Government, and destroyed, and at the same time, I would repeal the legal tender clause as to all debts contracted after that time." This is all that he has offered in reference to his method of resumption, yet he seems to imply something further to complete resumption, as he says: "The effect of that would be to make the condition *precedent* to a return to specie payments." And further: "Unless we make the conditions precedent, unless we fix the time certain in the future, the people will never prepare for it, and will never be more ready than to-day."

Now let us examine how this would work. The first point in the proposition is to bind and determine the action of a future Congress. This is pernicious policy, if it be anything more than a recommendation, as being contrary to the genius of our institutions, in presuming to dictate to the people what policy they may require to be pursued by their future representatives. In its financial aspect, how can it be known that the people will be any better prepared for resumption then than now; or that they will at that time wish to resume? If the Government hoard gold in sufficient quantity, *it* may be better prepared; but the people may not. Prices may remain on a range higher than gold, and the claim will be set up that to change from a currency to a gold basis, would involve a great reduction of prices. And this is foreseen and acknowledged by Mr. Jones, when he says: "This would be contraction, and would cause a reduction in the price of everything."

This is legislation with a view direct to change prices. The sophistry usually set up in defense of such legislation is, that all commodities and values being equally affected, there is no harm done. And it is because this is a *sophistry*, and not a *truth*, that there is irretrievable harm done by such legislation. It has been shown that there are greai-industries and great sections of country peculiarly susceptible to the reducing and paralyzing effects of a contracting currency, which not only have to bear their own proper share of the aggregate reduction of prices, but have to bear that portion which properly belongs to other industries, pursuits, interests, and forms of wealth, which are so in-

trenched behind defénses that they can resist and ward off
their share of the aggregate reduction.

The corollary of this is also true, with some modification,
during an era of inflation—that is, when the currency is increased in a ratio greater than that of the increase of population—that those industries, pursuits, callings, interests,
and forms of wealth, which I have classified as of fixed or
nearly fixed values, and which have the power to resist the
effects of a contracting currency, are the last to avail themselves of the effects of an expanding currency, as will be
seen when we reflect upon the nature of debts and credits—
loans on mortgages—leases—rents—salaries for terms—contracts extending over considerable time, insurance, taxes,
and those expenses and commodities whose prices become
conventional—and such things as these enter into as a large
element of cost.

Those industries the prices of whose products are most
flexible, are very susceptible to the earlier waves of an expanding currency. But when they have been carried to a
certain height, they find a limit by the laws of supply and
demand, through the operations of commerce. Rising prices
stimulate production, and the surplus must seek a foreign
market; and the foreign price (if the surplus be a considerable portion of the whole product), when converted into
currency through the gold premium, determines the price
of the whole product in the domestic market. When the
productive industries have drawn to their service as much
of the increasing volume of the currency as they can profitably employ, and their prices find their maximum limita-
tions, if the inflation continues as during the war, the redundancy of money continually finds new and enlarging
channels in which to flow—in the exchanging of increasing
products—in the increase of investments in the productive
industries, and in the more hazardous and speculative enterprises, and in investments in internal improvements—
the opening of mines—the establishment of new and untried
industries, speculations in real estate, stocks, etc.; and these
channels, which the increasing volume of currency first
makes, and then flows in, absorb the flood with an ever
widening capacity. And it is because it is an incident of

inflation, that after satisfying the wants of productive industry, the redundancy flows into more hazardous investments, and among them into Wall Street stock operations, that these operations have first been regarded as typical and representative of its general effects; and secondly, those effects, in whatever form of enterprise they appear, and however they have enriched and beautified the country, and however much they have added to the prosperity and resources of the people, and illustrated their genius, their energy and their enterprise, by an adroit and unwarrantable use of language, are designedly and flippantly, but unjustly, characterized by all the opprobrious epithets applied . to Wall Street operations.

Nothing herein, however, is designed to advocate an enlargement of the currency out of proportion to the growth of population. Such an increase would have objectionable effects, but the evil effects of such an increase would be magnified ten fold—yea, an hundred fold—by a contraction of like amount. During inflation, though there is a difference in the relative effects upon different industries and interests, yet all feel in a greater or less degree the buoyancy, hopefulness, and inspiration of the general prosperity; and there are but few, very few, of those whose interests are chiefly in the class of fixed values, who are not, to a greater or less extent, compensated through other interests, and who do not profit in common with others by the increased aggregate of actual wealth arising from the increased activity of all productive forces. While, during contraction, not only is there a different relative effect upon different industries and interests, but all feel in a greater or less degree its depressing and harassing effect, and the aggregate waste from enforced idleness and the obstruction to business, the stagnation of all the productive forces, and the sacrifices of property, and the losses, harassments and costs by the enforced settlement of accounts, cause an enormous loss of real wealth, which is sure to affect seriously and detrimentally even the most favored classes.

And here I reiterate that a specie base currency involves a constant ebb and flow of the quantity of currency in circulation, while an irredeemable currency can be continued in a fixed ratio to the population.

And, further, with a specie base currency every expansion
involves *necessarily a contraction.* While with our irredeemable currency *expansion* does not involve contraction, and
contraction only follows expansion when unwise legislation
promotes it or *permits it.* For this reason our irredeemable
currency in the late panic stood like a bulwark, to stay and
return the falling tide of prices. The panic was in nowise
attributable to the nature of the currency. It was the result of a shock to the public mind and business confidence
by the failure of a great banking house which had assumed
too great responsibilities in a special undertaking which
locked up its capital: which shock reacted upon and shook
the superstructure of the monetary system—of deposits and
loans, and bank and business credit—but the basis—the
currency—remained firm without depreciation in value or
diminution in quantity, and this incontractibility of the currency, either by depreciation or diminution, together with
the slight increase in quantity through the necessities of
the Government, is what so soon checked the panic and restored business confidence, and saved the country from incomparably greater business disaster and paralysis. Mr.
Jones proposes deliberately to legislate to bring about contraction, his end in view being to substitute a redeemable
for an irredeemable currency, which is the substitution of
a worse for a better currency ; a change to be avoided instead of being sought, even if it could be had without cost.

"On the day set the greenbacks should be redeemed
either in gold or in bonds at the option of the Government,
and destroyed." If the Government on and after the day
set is able to redeem all greenbacks presented in gold, the
gold board and gold premium would be at an end—currency
would be at par with gold, because greenbacks would be
redeemable in gold on demand. That would be what is
called "resumption." All business thenceforth would be
on a gold basis. Placing legal tenders upon a gold basis
or canceling them would place all business upon a gold basis. The national banks would be the first at the doors of
the Treasury demanding gold for their legal tender reserves,
and would not be slow in eliminating the legal tenders from
the volume of money passing through their hands and pre-

senting them for redemption. The gold they would obtain for their reserves would still be held as reserves; beyond that the gold received would be a.part of their active loanable capital, and after the exhaustion of their bank notes on hand would pass into circulation as loans, and their gold reserves would be drawn upon to redeem their notes and must be replenished. Thus gold would go into circulation to supply the place of greenbacks withdrawn from active circulation. The gold put into circulation would be of equal volume to the legal tenders withdrawn from circulation and destroyed. It may be asked, therefore, how can that be contraction and how can that disturb prices? Let us see.

The reduction and disturbance of prices would commence before, and continue after the day set for specie redemption. At a period six or eight months anterior to that day, let us suppose the premium on gold to be 15 per cent., and that prices of commodities were adjusted to this rate. Importations may be supposed to be reasonably profitable at the ruling prices, with a rebate to the importer of 15 per cent. for the conversion of currency into gold. With the same volume of currency, prices remain unchanged, except by demand and supply. The demand will be diminished by the attempt to prepare for resumption, by holders intermediate between producers and consumers endeavoring to sail under bare poles with light stocks, by selling all they can and buying as little as they can in anticipation of lower prices. Thus, each acting for himself, they conspire to a common end—the lessening of the demand and the lowering of prices. On the other hand, the supply will be increased by increased importations. Importers anticipating a decline of the gold premium, multiply their imports, to make as large sales as possible before the decline of prices. As the time approaches, if the gold premium remains high, currency will be hoarded and withdrawn from active circulation by those having to make payments abroad, as it becomes more profitable to await the day of redemption and conversion into gold. at par, than to lose the ruling high premium by present conversion. This lessens the demand for gold and helps to depress its price, and by contracting the active currency, as well as by the effect on gold, it depresses the prices of other commodities. The volume of imports increasing day by day, can be put upon the markets at steadily declining prices, and still preserve the ordinary profits, because the gold premium is day by day declining until it touches zero on the day of redemption. Gold, the most sensitive or flexible, is first in finding the gold base price.

The prices of other commodities linger behind at a greater or less remoteness, resisting the downward tendency with all the power of resistance they have, until they find a point in relation to the new status which they can maintain.

When prices have adjusted themselves to the gold base, it will be found that all those products which depend mainly or largely upon foreign markets, have suffered a decline of nominal value equal to the former gold premium. While products depending upon home markets in competition with imports will have declined less, because less directly affected, and because the tariff affords them a measure of defence.

It is obvious from the causes stated that the prices of exportable products and of products in competition with imports, would decline in consequence of the decline of the gold premium, while there would have been but a slight contraction of the currency—that of hoarding currency in anticipation of redemption—and the question may arise, how is it that such a fall of prices can occur without a corresponding contraction of the currency? The answer is to be found in the two principles before explained. 1st, that domestic prices will be determined in a great measure by the prices of surplus products seeking foreign markets. 2d, by the commercial distribution of the currency.

The proportion of the common currency which a commodity can draw to its service is in ratio to the quantity and price of the commodity. Whatever depresses its price forces it to relinquish a portion of the currency it controled under the higher price, and that portion is not merely free to flow, but is forced into other channels of employment, because the channels it has been flowing in, having been compressed, cannot hold it. If there be channels of legitimate enterprise and industry open and ready to re-

ceive it, it flows into them; but if not, it finds the channsel
of the class of more hazardous investments, (stock speculations, real estate investments, etc.,) whose capacity to
absorb is as elastic as the nominal values floated upon them.
Hence the volume of currency released from the service of
productive industries by a decline of prices, flows directly
into the channels of speculative investments, and is
absorbed by the rising tide of nominal values therein; and
this portion of the common currency will continue to be
diverted to this service, until it shall be forced out of it by
a further contraction of the circulating medium, which
would follow the redemption of greenbacks in gold.

It will be found, therefore, that one of the effects of a return to a gold-base currency, as recommended by Senator
Jones, will be, for a time at least, to increase the "mania"
for "gambling" in stocks.

In grouping the classes of property of fixed values, debts
and credits are included, and, consequently, the relation of
debtor and creditor, and I might, therefore, proceed without further consideration of this relation, but its importance
merits further attention. Whenever the Government re-
deems its greenbacks in gold, every debt and obligation in the
country is placed upon a gold basis. The magnitude of the
amount of debts and liabilities and accruing obligations
cannot be told. And the fixedness of value of this vast
amount of money of account is little appreciated in the dis-
cussions of the financial problem. Most persons are at the
same time both debtors and creditors, and the same may be
said of the respective sections of the country. Each is a
debtor or creditor as his or its excess is debt or credit.

The excess only of debt or credit can be affected by a
change of currency values: but this excess amounts to billions of dollars, and affects differently sections in the same
manner as it affects differently individuals. And the burden
of all indebtedness is greatly magnified by contraction and
change of basis of price, and the purchasing power of the
creditor's demand, is enhanced in the same ratio. How
does this harmonize with the Hon. Senator's moral and political ethics as announced and heretofore quoted, viz: "No
government, no people, can be prosperous that ignores the

proposition that honesty is the best policy, that, by any sort of legislation, disturbs the relationship between debtor and creditor?"

During expansion, the creditor, who is relatively injured, may not be, and seldom is, positively injured thereby. As has been shown, he is often compensated in many ways, and is benefited by the general increased activity and prosperity.

During contraction, on the other hand, though he may be benefited relative to the debtor, he may be, and almost invariably is positively injured, by sharing, to a greater or less extent, the common loss resulting from stagnation of business and bankruptcy. The burden of debt may crush the debtor, but the creditor cannot shield himself from all harm. The positive evil to one is not a positive benefit to the other. The evils of expansion in reference to the relation of debtor and creditor are like those of a summer shower which may moisten some ungarnered hay, but which is a general blessing. While the evils of contraction in reference to this relation are like the sweeping blasts of a tornado at sea that strews its pathway with blighted lives and the wrecks of human hope and endeavor.

As there are individuals and industries whose status is constantly that of debtor or creditor, so there are large sections which usually or constantly hold to each other these relations. And not only is it not derogatory to the debtor sections, but they reflect credit upon their courage in assuming such obligations, to give opportunity to their industry and their enterprise; and it is unworthy of exalted station to reproach that status with obloquy, by designating it as the result of gambling and reckless speculation.

I have thus far considered Senator Jones' plan of resumption on the hypothesis that, on the day appointed for redemption, the government would have hoarded sufficient gold to respond to the demand, and redeem all greenbacks in gold. But the plan pre-supposes that the government will not be able to do this, or, if able to redeem in gold, it may be inexpedient to do so. Therefore a redemption with an option is proposed. Redemption with an option is not original with Mr. Jones. It has been long enough before the Senate to have its merits canvassed; and it is surprising that it should be repeatedly presented as *a method of redemption*. To redeem legal tenders in gold, is redemption, as commonly understood. To refuse to redeem in gold, after that had been commenced, would be suspension. To offer a bond instead of gold, is to suspend specie payments and to offer a merchantable article at a fixed price. Nothing is said of the interest such bonds should bear. If the interest be five per cent., and their sale value in foreign markets be less than par—two or more per cent.—they would be refused. This would necessitate the continuance of the Gold Board— and there would be a gold premium so long as the government should refuse to redeem in gold and offer bonds that were worth less than gold in the market; and the value of the bonds would react upon and limit the premium on gold. If, on the other hand, the interest on these bonds be placed high enough to make their home market price, gauged by their foreign market price, worth more than gold when gold is at par with legal tenders, then the demand would be constantly for bonds which would be withheld so long as there was gold to redeem with; and those applicants for redemption would be the most fortunate whose greenbacks would command bonds. We are thus conducted to the following conclusions:

1st. That the interest on the bonds must be such a rate as to make them worth par or more than par in gold in our market or they will not be accepted except in preference to gold at a premium.

2d. That though the interest be gauged to make them at par with gold, financial perturbations at home or abroad might depress them below par, when they would become unacceptable, and therefore unavailable so long as their market price renders them undesirable.

3d. The exchange and cancellation of greenbacks for bonds, in whatever amount, would be a direct contraction of the currency to that amount.

4th. The uncertainty of the value of the bonds and of the continuance of redemption in gold, would continue the gold market, and gold premium, and might result in a constant alternation of resumption and suspension of specie payments.

5th. That redemption in gold by preventing the payment of a portion of the national interest-debt, or redemption in bonds by increasing our national interest-debt, would impose a new burden upon the nation of more than twenty millions of dollars annually.

Mr. Jones proposes to repeal the legal tender clause. If redemption in gold on and after the day appointed is to be a success, this is very much like hanging a man and then issuing a decree to prevent him from exercising his civil functions.

If greenbacks are redeemable in gold, and at par with gold, or thereabout, in the transactions of business, they will remain a part of the currency until entirely absorbed, and will be used in the settlement of accounts, even those settled under judgments of courts, as bank bills are now, though not enforced by the courts, and the legal tender clause would have no practical effect.

But if redemption in gold is not to be a success, then to repeal the legal tender clause would be a violation of the public good faith.

When the legal tenders were issued, had the Government been able to redeem them on demand in gold, there is no reason to believe that they would have been made legal-tender. But because this could not be done, they were made legal-tender, that those who were under the necessity of receiving them in settlement of accounts might in turn pay them in settlement of accounts; hence their withdrawal and cancellation, *only*, can cancel this attribute without a breach of faith.

I have endeavored to show, and I think successfully, that to change from our irredeemable currency basis to a gold-base currency and specie payments would be detrimental to the best interests of the whole country; and I submit that the increased interest burden necessitated by Senator Jones' plan of resumption (or indeed by any plan) is but a small part of the increased burdens, the end of which no man can see, that would inevitably follow, particularly in view of the fact that we have a large amount of foreign indebtedness to pay, interest and principal, and that by the change proposed we virtually agree to transport our exportable products from the center to the shores of our continent and across the ocean to the shores of other continents to be placed upon foreign markets, to be sold at their prices, virtually paying all costs and risks of transit, though the profits of transportation be reaped by foreign commerce, to obtain the money necessary to pay our foreign indebtedness. In other words, we pay them in our products, and transport these products to their doors and accept what they, under the laws of trade, choose to give us for them. This is the feast to which we are invited.

A strong pressure is brought in the discussion of this question to impress upon the public mind that there is a present imperative and irremovable obligation on the part of the Government to redeem the legal tenders in gold coin. This obligation is based upon the words on the face of the legal tenders—"The United States will pay to the bearer" or "promise to pay to the bearer" the number of dollars designated. These phrases are stigmatized as Government lies, as "dishonored promises," "promises issued with a deliberate intention to break them"—"that they are not money, but lies." These epithets are applied to our national currency by a moral light and guide in the land, one endowed with divine erudition—the head of the Divinity School in one of the most influential and venerable institutions of learning—one who, in the exercise of his exalted sentiments and refined and elegant taste, speaks of the majority of the members of Congress as "simpletons"—"or, if not simpletons, then knaves."* The Church,† too, in some instances, is engaged in denouncing the immorality of our national currency. The resumptionists appear to have exhausted their arguments on the basis of the laws of trade and finance, and also their patience, and now are calling to their aid the force of their moral enginery to shock and arouse the conscience of the nation, to induce a course of policy which they apprehend will not be sanctioned by an appeal to its intelligence on the basis of its monetary interests.

---

* See letter of Rev. Dr. Bacon, of Yale, to Hon. W. W. Phelps, M. C., N. Y. *Tribune.*
† Fast-Day Sermon of *Rev.* Dr. Bartol.

There is no denial of the promise, but its present demand is of the nature of a demand for a pound of flesh—the flesh to be taken from the party making the demand.

A. has a horse to sell. He offers him for ninety dollars in gold, or one hundred dollars in currency. B. purchases the horse, and will pay ninety dollars in gold, if insisted upon, or one hundred dollars in currency. To avoid the inconvenience to B. of converting currency into gold, and to A. of reconverting gold into currency when he comes to exchange his money for commodities, A. accepts—indeed, prefers—currency. A. sees on the face of the currency a "promise to pay."

Now do the equities of Divinity Schools teach that A. has a righteous claim for a hundred dollars in gold? And if he demands it, is his demand in accordance with Divine equity? Did he not demand and receive ten dollars in currency more than the value of his horse in gold, *because* the Government was unprepared, or, if you please, refused, or, what is better, deemed it inexpedient to redeem its currency in gold? And was not the receipt of those ten dollars a waiver of his claim to payment in gold? And has he a Divine moral right to retain those ten dollars, and to the redemption of his full amount of currency in gold, dollar for dollar? And if Professors of Divinity teach the affirmative of the first of these questions, to whom is applicable the epithets "simpletons," or, if not simpletons, then "knaves?"

If A has no equitable right to demand a hundred dollars in gold for the currency he received for his horse, then how is the Government under obligation to pay *him* a hundred dollars in gold for that currency. And is the Government's honor irretrievably lost if it refuses to violate equity to carry out a technical promise?

Does A persist in his demand for gold redemption? The Government replies that it is not prepared, but if A will submit to be taxed one hundred dollars in gold, or will authorize it to obtain a loan in his name of one hundred dollars bearing interest, which he must pay in increased taxation, and a majority of his fellow citizens unite with him in a like demand under like conditions, it will obey their behests, as their humble servant, and that whatever it

does, must be done in their name and at their cost, and if a
majority of his fellow citizens refuse to join in his demand
for gold redemption at such unavoidable costs, are they to
be stigmatized as repudiators seeking their country's dis-
honor? or as "simpletous" "or if not simpletons, knaves?"
And is A whose avarice seeks to increase the purchasing
power of his hundred dollars of currency through resumption and increased national taxation, the man to stand upon
a pedestal as a model of honesty and honor, while he points
the finger of scorn at his fellow citizens as dishonorable
repudiators?

The gold to be paid to the people must be furnished by
the people, and when the burden has been changed from
one shoulder to the other, it will be found to be augmented
by the interest on increased interest bearing-national debt.
And this obligation or promise being from the people to
the people, the people have a moral right to determine
what policy they will pursue, so long as they make no
invidious distinctions against individuals or classes.

The burdens of taxation would not fall upon individuals
in the ratio of the money they held for redemption. Therein would be the greater injustice. Those whose wealth was
in the form of currency and currency demands would be
immediate, or at least relative, gainers by the policy of redemption, while their gains would be added to the other
burdens of redemption in gold, to be borne by those whose
wealth or interests were in other forms; and eventually all
classes would suffer by the mal-policy of redemption.

The currency valued as an investment.

The article in the *North American Review*, Jan., 1874,
before referred to, assumes that the value of the currency is
not indicated by the gold premium, that is purely acci-
dental; that its true value cannot be determined, because it
is not known when it will be redeemed; that if the Government should determine to redeem its currency in gold in
1884, its value might readily be computed by finding the
value of a note running ten years to maturity. This hypothesis, computing at six per cent., simple interest, gives
sixty-two and half per cent. as the value of currency, or a

5

gold premium of sixty per cent. instead of twelve to fifteen per cent. as at present. Compound interest would make the difference still greater.

How can it be sanely assumed that the currency is only worth sixty-two and a half per cent. in gold because the government should postpone redemption ten years, when it can be converted into eighty-eight per cent. of gold, by simply going into the market for that purpose?

The hypothesis proceeds upon the assumption that a government note is an investment, and not currency: and that its current convertible value depends upon the time of its redemption, and not upon the fact that, nominal commercial values are adjusted to the quantity of currency (as stated in the article referred to) and that the price of gold, like that of all other commodities, is adjusted by demand and supply, and regulated to the currency and the prices of all other commodities, through the gold premium.

By converting currency into an investment a part of its value (as a currency) is destroyed. On the same supposition, if a hundred dollars in gold were locked up as an investment to remain ten years, three eighths of its present value would be destroyed at a computation at simple interest: and this would be but little more absurd than to lock up as an investment, currency convertible into eighty-eight or ninety per cent. of gold, and keep it locked up ten years till the day set for redemption, in order to prove that its present true value is only five eighths of its nominal value.

It may be replied on the hypothesis under consideration, that if the date of redemption were set ten years hence, that thereupon currency could not be converted into eighty-eight per cent. of gold—that the gold premium would rise, and the convertibility of currency into gold would sink in the ratio of the discount of a personal note having ten years to run without interest.

This reply, like the hypothesis itself, is a groundless assumption. It comes from regarding the currency as a debt of the government, and that its current value depends upon the credit which each recipient extends to the government's debt, and that it is a forced loan from the people to the government; and from *disregarding* the uses and nature of

currency as a currency, its power to measure values, to effect
exchanges and to settle accounts; and that it has a current
value which is at all times convertible into intrinsic value in
every desirable form of purchasable commodities or interests, including gold itself, at prices measured in the aggregate by its volume, like all other currencies which consum-
mate payments, and at respective relative prices as the
various commodities and interests are affected relatively by
the laws of trade; and by entertaining the idea that nothing
is payment that is not a transfer of intrinsic value.

I meet the assumption by a counter assertion, based upon
the general laws of trade governing currencies and our irredeemable currency in particular, that were Congress to
resolve to not redeem the currency in less than ten years
and make no guaranty to redeem it then, that such policy
would not affect the gold premium two per cent. unless,
perhaps, spasmodically for a week or two, when it would
regain its equilibrium.

If the currency were a debt of the government to the people, and a forced loan from the people, the government being only an agency of the people, its debts are their debts,
and in reference to the currency they are debtors and creditors, and the account is balanced.

The currency is neither a debt nor a loan, but an instrumentality of business, by creating which the government
saved to the people the necessity of issuing four hundred
millions of interest-bearing bonds, and was enabled to
facilitate the sale of the lessened amount it was necessary
to issue. And a saving to the people of the interest on
bonds equal to the amount of legal tender currency will
continue so long as they use it as a currency.

When the legal tenders were first issued it is probable
every man who voted for them regarded them as a temporary currency to supply a temporary want, and it was not
the intention to issue a permanently irredeemable currency.
And it is very probable that it was not the intention to
change the basis of the circulating medium; and had it
been a non-legal tender, like all former issues of paper
money, it could not have changed the basis of the currency,
it could not have been the *par* of values, it could not have

been kept at par in effecting exchanges or in the settlement, of accounts, but would immediately have sunk to a discount, and would have been subject to all the vicissitudes of the continental currency of the Revolution, but by being made a legal tender that its recipients from the Government, directly or remotely, should be enabled to pass it as they had been forced to receive it, at par in the settlement of accounts, it became immediately the basis of all accounts and all values: and the State banks changed the basis of their circulation from gold to legal tender because they were enabled to redeem their promises in legal tenders instead of gold. The law of Congress making Government issues a legal tender, the law of finance placed all accounts, all values, and consequently all business on that basis, and gold was demonetized, and the quantity of gold in a gold dollar became worth more than a dollar by currency measure of values. When the Government issued the legal tenders it could not redeem them in gold on demand. If it could have done so it would not have made them legal tenders, because every one receiving them would have had his protection against loss by demanding redemption in gold. The Government did not promise to pay on demand. In lieu of this, and as an equivalent protection, it made its issues legal tenders. This changed the nature of its issues from that of a loan and debt to that of a currency.

A loan presupposes the transfer or withholding of *active capital* from the loanor, to, or by the loanee, and whenever a loan is effected a rate of interest is guaranteed the loanor as a recompense for the loss by the detention of *active capital*, and when no interest is guaranteed the loss is suffered by a discount in the market value of the debt. This inheres in the nature of a loan, by the laws of finance and business.

The issuance of the currency is not a detention or abstraction of active capital from the people or from the individuals to whom it is issued. It is itself active capital. It may be said that it draws no interest and yields no profit while it is held in hand. The same is the case with gold coin, or any currency. A hundred dollars in gold will yield no man a profit so long as he keeps it in his pocket; when it is currency, and not a commodity. He can only be profited by it by parting with it. If it becomes interest-bearing, and made profitable to hold, it is impaired as a currency, and becomes an investment in the ratio that its interest approaches the ordinary profits of investments.

On the hypothesis that the currency is only a non-interest paying debt, and a forced loan from the people, why is it that every man who has an audited certified claim against the Government is desirous to cancel his claim by the receipt of currency payment? On this hypothesis he would only have changed the form of his claim; he would not have received payment. *Why so universal a desire to obtain so small a result?* It is because the hypothesis is false. When a man holds a valid claim against the Government, he can only convert it into active capital by a discount proportionate to the current rate of interest for the time that will probably elapse before the Government will make payment in currency — and when he has converted it, he only receives currency (another form of claim, so called, against the Government). He suffers the discount, because he can thereby change his non-active capital (claim) into active capital (currency)—and the purchaser of the claim makes an investment of active capital, and receives the discount as a compensation for the detention of his active capital until the payment of the claim; when his active capital is restored to him.

The conclusion is therefore inevitable, that a loan cannot be made from the people or from individuals to the Government, without a surrender of active capital; and therefore the Government does not obtain a loan from the people by furnishing a currency for the people.

A non-interest bearing claim against the Government, in the hands of the claimant, is a species of non-active capital. By its payment in currency, and cancelation, it is converted into active capital, and *that is payment.* The claim is canceled, the account is closed and balanced, and ultimated and consummated in fact and in law, and *that is payment.*

The non-active capital in the claim has been converted into active capital in the possession and ownership of the claimant, and is convertible at will into every form of intrinsic value, including gold, and into every desirable form of possession in the civilized world by virtue of its currency properties within our own country, and through the laws of trade and commerce elsewhere. And thus the possessor has his payment. And whenever he exchanges his currency for any purchasable article, or for any object whatever, at his option, *that is redemption* to him. The people who issued it to him through their government have kept their faith, and redeemed it. And so long as the legal tenders remain unimpaired as a currency, the promise to pay is not an obligation on demand. But whenever the Government impairs them as a currency by repealing the legal tender clause, or otherwise, the promise to pay will become an obligation, and will be redeemed in good faith.

The good faith of the nation in the event of the impairment or extinction of the currency, would be as imperatively bound to protect the holders against loss, if the words "promise to pay" were not on the face of the notes; and any Congress which the American people shall elect will have sense and conscience and interest and consideration enough not to disregard that obligation. The promissory phrases are unnecessary to the legal tenders as a currency, and might be omitted without impairment, as they are omitted from the fractional currency, which no one believes is less protected by the good faith of the government on that account. And irritable and egotistical Doctors of Divinity may rest assured that the honor of the Nation rests not solely upon their shoulders, even if the increase by resumption of the purchasing power of their salaries shall be indefinitely postponed.

RESUMÉ.

I have endeavored to show that "resumption of specie payments," does not guarantee steadiness of business, and that it is in no sense a sound financial basis, but on the contrary presupposes ebbs and flows of the currency base from and to our country through the laws of commerce—continual alternations of contraction and expansion of the currency, and rising and falling tides of prices, detrimental to business and business equities, causing us in our commercial relations to "buy dear and sell cheap;" and that our irredeemable currency maintained in a constant ratio to the population, is attended with contrary and desirable results, and affords the best guaranty against these evils.

And that the gold premium has become the best indicator of the business status and prospect; and that a rising premium indicates increasing business activity, and a falling premium indicates a shrinkage of prices and business obstruction. And that the business indications of the balance of trade, and the rate of foreign exchange under a gold base currency, *have been reversed by our irredeemable currency.*

I have also endeavored to show that the great amount of national, state and municipal bonds and investment securities held by our people at the close of the war, and those since issued, inevitably flow to European markets, from the great amount of accumulating capital seeking investment there at lower rates of interest than are usually obtained in this country; and that the exportation of these securities would have taken place under any system of finance.

Under a gold base currency it would have tended to accumulate gold like an excess of any kind of exportations, which would have served to increase banking capital and enlarge the bank circulation, which would have continued to expand until the exportation of securities would have been checked by exhaustion, and its culmination would have been followed by a panic and business paralysis such as the country has never experienced, not even in 1837.

And that under our irredeemable currency, the exportation of these securities has had a depressing effect upon general business—first, and in the greatest measure, by direct competition with our exportable products, and secondly, by facilitating importations, in direct competition with many domestic industries and interests ; but this depressing effect has been modified, though far from fully compensated, by the increased prosperity, experienced in those countries from which we have largely imported, and thereby widened the demand and kept up the gold prices for our exports in their markets. That this cause of depression being wholly or nearly exhausted, its exhaustion will bring relief to those great industries and sections that have been deleteriously affected by it. And that the payment of the interest, or the principal at maturity or before, will have a stimulating and reviving effect upon business, and will be an inconsiderable burden and easily borne under the inspiration and buoyancy of guaranteed business prosperity.

And that instead of our foreign indebtedness and foreign credit being a source of constant anxiety and alarm, causing business perturbations, as they would be under a gold base currency, subject to every monetary contingency and every foreign or international complication, and the friendship or animosity of the leaders of public opinion abroad, under our irredeemable currency we are utterly independent of these considerations, because a diminution of our foreign credit and return of our securities for payment or purchase will be a direct cause of business prosperity and rejoicing; and this gives us a masterly business status in reference to all questions of international diplomacy. And that the distribution of the currency has been peculiarly affected by the cause that has depressed the currency prices of exportable products, adversely to great industries, interests and sections, and that the exhaustion of this cause will restore to those industries, interests and sections a due and adequate share of the common currency.

These are the main points I have attempted to elucidate.

My comments on the speech of Senator Jones are not so much intended to controvert the tenor of his statements of facts, though he indulges in hyperbole, as to call attention to the fallacies of his reasoning, conclusions and propositions, and to direct attention to the true cause of the financial and commercial phenomena of which he complains, and to show that they are not attributable to our irredeemable currency, and would only be aggravated by resumption. And my comments upon the letter of Rev. Dr. Bacon are intended as a defense, however feeble, against the animadversions upon our country's currency, statesmen and national honor of a growing throng who assume superior airs, and who, having exhausted their logic and their patience, avail themselves of the opportunity to issue their reserves of detraction.

Trusting that this brief contribution to the general discussion of the financial problem may not prove altogether valueless, I commend it to the attention and candid consideration of my fellow-citizens.

www.ingramcontent.com/pod-product-compliance
Lightning Source LLC
Chambersburg PA
CBHW021530270326
41930CB00008B/1177